MW00814570

MY DADDY'S PROMISE

Dave,
Friendship over
been begins the
brewing of lifelong
bonds

MY DADDY'S PROMISE

LESSONS LEARNED THROUGH CAREGIVING

CARL W. KENNEY II

Copyright © 2020 by Carl W. Kenney II

All rights reserved.

No part of this book may be reproduced in any form or by any electronic or mechanical means, including information storage and retrieval systems, without written permission from the author, except for the use of brief quotations in a book review.

Dedicated to King T. Kenney, Lenise T. Kenney, Krista T. Kenney and Julian T. Kenney.

My mentor Dr. Walter Daniels, first black vice-chancellor at the University of Missouri, used to say, "the goal of life is for the offspring to spring further than the spring sprang".

Spring beyond my dreams.

FOREWORD

Every word from the pen of Carl Kenney is inviting and captivating. It is the prose of a master storyteller as if he is alone with you in having a most intimate conversation that will lift you to emotional highs and descending depths of teary lows. The narrative is packed with wisdom as he narrates with meticulous detail what life was like for his father in rural and small-town Missouri during the days of state sponsored segregation.

His father weathered the ugly times with dignity that were designed to dehumanize him. Carl Kenney, with great skill, introduces the coping mechanisms that were the instruments of survival his father and our ancestors used as champions of their plight. He also shares the lessons to be learned from the elders.

This wonderful book is a stereotype breaker of a myth that is normalized by the opinion makers of America life. The opinion makers paint a negative picture of the rolling stone black father who is despised by his son. Carl shares the unending love between him and his father and how, at the top of his career in Durham North Carolina, he was motivated by love to give status and hard-earned security to return to Columbia, Missouri to be a caregiver for his dad. Nothing prepares one for caregiving. One does not know what to expect as a caregiver, and one does not have any idea what caregiving burnout is until one experiences it.

The book is required reading for caregiving. Being highly schooled in theology and religious studies, Carl shares that textbook religion does not sustain one in crisis or in confronting death dealing challenges or in facing encounters with unexplained evil. He helps the reader to ponder his/her own predicament and faith issues. The book is essential reading for anyone suffering with grief.

Brother Carl is nakedly honest and transparent in sharing his weaknesses and strengths, and the help that he should have had from the so-called helping institutions of society. While being open and honest about white supremacy being alive and well in Missouri, it was hopeful and encouraging to learn that a predominantly white American Baptist Church with a female pastor opened wide the doors of the church for his father's home going celebration without charging the $500.00 fee the African American church of which his father had been a long time giving member wanted.

There are multi-layers if meanings in the book that I have not shared. But this book gave me deeper insight into the loving heart and beautiful mind of the author who follows Jesus more nearly, loves others more dearly and articulates the meaning of faith in *My Daddy's Promise.*

J. Alfred. Smith. Sr., pastor emeritus of Allen Temple Baptist Church in Oakland, California and professor emeritus at American Baptist Seminary of the West.

PREFACE

"All these years I thought I trained your mama. Woke up this morning and figured out she trained me" -Carl W. Kenney, Sr. (November 7, 1936 – May 24, 2015)

My next book is titled <u>My Mama's Freedom.</u> I mention it here because of the importance of correlating my daddy's impact on my life with my mama's continued presence in making me a better man. The telling of my mama's story demands a focus on her unique contribution. There is nothing like the strength and determination of black women. That story is coming soon.

I acknowledge my mama along with the aunts and uncles, most of whom are dead, who fueled in me a desire to walk this earth like my presence deserves attention. My faith journey has exposed me to the power of ancestors. Like the Bible's affirmation of "the mighty cloud of witnesses", I believe my ancestors are watching over me.

Some made their way to America via the Middle Passage. They were part of the group of millions of Africans forcibly transported to what their enslavers claimed to be the New World. I'm conscious of my ancestors who didn't make it from the coast of Africa to a port of disembarkation. Some died onboard a ship. Others jump into the Atlantic Ocean proclaiming a desire to die before being a slave.

I hear and feel my ancestors prodding me to hold on, just a little while longer. I see them in the faces of my children – King, Lenise and Krista. I'm reminded of our call to form a village for all children in claiming Julian as my son. The love of our ancestors is reflected in our willingness to rename what it means to be family. In renaming, we reclaim everything taken away – our culture, our language, our religion, our families, our very lives – with bold pronouncements that "this joy that we have, the world didn't give it and the world can't take it away.

I acknowledge the strength of our collective family. This too is my daddy's promise. It's the passage of a will to transcend all forms of brokenness in celebration of a life and love untarnished by all weapons formed against us. Yes, all of it will pass to rekindle the enchantment of our collective dreams.

I acknowledge our dreams.

My daddy's spirit wrote this book. Each word is a musing of his being. My ambition is to convey the essence of his sustained witness. My daddy lives in and through this book. His continued unrelenting presence grants each of us the audacity to believe we are never alone. Those ancestors keep watching over us declaring a life of vast possibilities.

This is my mama's story. This is my sister Sandra's story. This story belongs to my children and their children. This story will be carried long after my death as a reminder of promises uttered during the Middle Passage.

This story was written with the support of friends who carried me during and after caregiving. Thanks praying women – Deborah Dalton, Rev. Muriel Johnson, Dr Cassandra Gould, Traci Kleekamp-Wilson, Rev. Aundreia Alexander, Dr. Cyndi Smith Frisby, Rev. Bonnie Cassida, Lisa Lynnette, Dani Moore, Rev. Richelle James, Dr. Melissa Harris-Perry, Brandi Jackson, Connie Companaro, Gwen Banks, Lois Deloatch, Evonne Coleman, Rev. Willetta J. Ar-Rahmann, Rev. Karen Georgia A. Thompson, Rev. Connie Pope, Sydney Carlson, Rev. Tonetta Killens Liz Jackson and Dr. Beverley Horvit – for keeping me grounded after my daddy's death.

I can never forget the love and support of Carl's Angels – Betty J. Redwood, Glenda D. Jones and Janice Webster – for holding my hands as my daddy transitioned.

Thanks to my inner circle of brothers – Dr. C. W. Dawson, Jr., Victor Moore, Steve Weinberg, Lennis Harris, Omar Beasley, Carl Webb, Sterling Freeman, Victor Hughes, Michael Palmer, Sherrod Banks, Dr. Starsky Wilson, Dante James, C. Jeffery Wright, Brett Chambers, Larry Crane, Dr. William-Hazel Height, Dr. Robert C. Scott, Dr. Howard John Wesley, Dr. Craig S. Keener, Dr. Gregory Hardy, Dr. J. Kameron Carter, Dr. Harmon Smith, Dr. Willie Jennings – for consistent presence and for teaching what it means to be faithful when the wind blows too strong to stand alone.

To the members of St. Paul United Methodist Church in Newton, North Carolina for providing a place for me to write; the members of Bethel Church in Columbia, Missouri for giving me a place to preach and to host my daddy's funeral; the members of Compassion Ministries of Durham for loving your pastor no matter what happens and the members of my Saturday Morning Breakfast Club for reminding me of why there's no place like Durham, North Carolina.

Thanks to the owners of the places where I write: Lakota Coffee Company and Dunn Brothers Coffee in Columbia, Missouri; Bean Traders Coffee, Cocoa Cinnamon, Joe Van Gogh, Beyú Caffé and Mad Hatter's Café and Bake Shop in Durham, North Carolina; Wisk & Barel, the Catawba Museum of History in Newton, North Carolina.

Don't forget my team: Maya Jackson, of The Jaxton Creative Group, for laying out my marketing vision; Jeff Poe, creative at Phunco, for designing the book cover; Chrystal Kelly, of Shattering Light Photography, for images that tell our story; Dr. Trevy A. McDonald, author of the novels, Round 'Bout Midnight and Time Will Tell and owner of Reyomi Publishing, LLC, for consulting on the publication of this book.

I told you it's a collective vision.

"I'm your daddy now," Dr. J. Alfred Smith, Sr., pastor emeritus of Allen Temple Baptist Church in Oakland, California, told me during the American Baptist Home Mission Societies *Space for Grace* conference held in Los Angeles, California in 2015. It was shortly after my father's death when Dr. Smith's words penetrated the part of me that needs assurance that I will not have to endure what followed alone.

Dr. Smith has been the daddy I need when life makes me wanna holla. When I asked him to write the foreword, he did not hesitate. What he wrote fortified my confidence in the words I placed on paper.

So, this is a book about us – all of us. Some of the names are left off these pages, but they too are a part of the village that makes <u>My Daddy's Promises</u> an open cannon of an enduring witness of a love between a father and his son. Our stories are linked in the celebration of lessons learned in life and death.

Listen for the silence. My daddy is whispering in the wind.

DOWN BY THE RIVERSIDE

My daddy was a storyteller. He was a repository of my family's traditions. He taught lesson regarding life before Civil Rights legislation and integration made it easier for black folks to overcome.

Time has taught me the lessons of my daddy's stories. They're the gifts that give witness to promises handed down through generations – his parents, grandparents and the ancestors he never met. My daddy's lessons are bursting with promises felt long after his death. They belong to me, my children, grandchildren and the descendants I will never meet.

Daddy's death has radically shifted the way I think about God and spirituality. I often hear my daddy speak to me. Sometimes, during a season of extended darkness, I hear and feel his presence – guiding me, loving me and reminding me nothing is too hard for God. Sometimes, it's after a sip of coffee while listening to one of his favorite songs. Maybe Sam Cooke, Ray Charles or James Cleveland singing "Peace Be Still."

My daddy's presence conjures in me the faith of my ancestors who carry the hope of life beyond these tears. My daddy's stories unwrap the oral tradition of a family made stronger by a will to overcome. The lack of written historical documentation is balanced whenever the Griot declares lessons about family and determination. My daddy's stories countered dehumanizing messages about being the property of white people who had no reason to believe black lives matter.

He didn't leave much money, but his stories are a reminder of what the world can't take away. I found strength and determination by listening to narratives about how my family depended on each other to survive. The strength is in making things work. The determination is in refusing to give up.

If an inheritance is a promise to enrich the quality of life of the beneficiary, my daddy's stories are my inheritance. My daddy continued the African story-telling tradition by talking about his bond with nature. His last days were animated in his quest to share what I hadn't heard before becoming his caregiver.

My daddy summoned the memory of his mother and father, grand-mother and grandfather, combined with life lessons attended to set me free. Free from what? The bondage that comes with the failure to comprehend what it all means.

All of it. The emotions stirred by being covered in black skin. The blues howling in my soul when others fail to understand my pain. The misery swallowed up in the bottom of a bottle and the tears pouring upon witnessing my wife and children wanting more than I could give.

My caregiving began a journey back to where it all began. My daddy's stories filled in the gaps that left me feeling too much was missing. These were the stories left out of books informing the white interpretation of American history. My daddy taught lessons told in both words and deeds. Some stories are best told without words.

You learn to feel the lesson by listening to how a body moves. Those lessons are the fulfillment of unspoken promises about doing all you can to help a son fulfill his dreams.

There are lessons about assumptions that reflect barriers stirred by generational differences. My beliefs regarding what I perceived as my daddy's weakness failed to consider the conditions he endured.

There are lessons about things lost. Some of the loss involves what we witness in others. A lot of it is about misery caused by what it takes to become a caregiver.

There are lessons about things gained as a result of caregiving. There are lessons involving the affirmation of a new identity after the

Griot dies leaving you with a lifetime of lessons filled with unexplored promises.

There are lessons trapped in memories. They are an inheritance produced by generational experiential wealth. They gush into my soul to evoke hope within the context of America's unfulfilled dream. My desire for white affirmation left me bankrupt after avoiding the capital of my daddy's lessons. My search for becoming more hid the blessing under the family tree.

My daddy's death is a lesson. His death began a journey in understanding promises black men hold in their hearts for sons in need of a joy the world can't take away.

I can't say that enough.

2

PROMISES

M y daddy talked a lot about days when fishing and hunting filled the space between the two jobs he maintained to provide for his wife and children.

Decades lapsed slowly as he dreamed of returning to the place where his body was strong enough to endure the footsteps needed to sit by the river.

My daddy was born on November 7, 1936 in

McBaine, Missouri. My granddaddy, James "Timber" Kenney, Sr., pulled up in a boat one day as the water from the Missouri River flooded the area near the home he made for his wife and children. My grandmama, Eula Lee, and their six children, James Jr., Elizabeth, Nokomis, Corine, Stanley and my daddy, were on the roof when the water crested. My granddaddy moved his family to Rocheport, Missouri where he made a living farming and making moonshine.

Before being forced to get in that boat, my daddy and his siblings learned to read and write in a one-room schoolhouse near the river. My granddaddy never learned to read, but he had the type of smarts black people needed to maneuver in a world with rules that made it difficult for black people to succeed.

They lived in a house built long before indoor plumbing and electricity. Going to the bathroom required a trip to the outhouse not far from the shack they called home. The sound of flying bugs was worsened by a smell that made me want to vomit. Grandma gave me a bucket at night because it was too dark outside, and no one knew what might be lurking near the outhouse.

My granddaddy's house had a well hidden beneath the wood planks that served the dual purpose of a front porch. The rope attached to the bucket took a long time to reach the bottom. The water was cold enough not to need ice in the Summer. I had nightmares about falling in the well and not being able to get out because I didn't know how to swim.

A bunch of old cars were parked around the house. Most of them didn't work. I remember getting locked in the trunk of a 1940-something Oldsmobile while playing hide and seek with my cousins. It happened when my grandma was cooking dinner on the wood stove in that hot kitchen. There was no air conditioner to moderate the heat during those Dog Days of Summer.

Caregiving teaches lessons about things aren't like they used to be.

My daddy learned numerous lessons from living in that house built between World War II and the Korean War. I learned some of those lessons whenever my daddy, mama, two sister and I made the 20-mile trip from Columbia, Missouri, where I was born and raised, to visit my grandparents near the Missouri River. I thought a lot about my ancestors working in the fields when my daddy forced me to pull weeds on the family farm. One day my daddy gave me a good whipping because I told him I was too tired and hot to pull weeds. The force of his black belt across my back and legs made me think about the lessons involving black people receiving punishment for attempting to run away.

Caregiving teaches lessons about being thankful you didn't live back then.

That old house told a story about survival. The life my daddy made for his family was built on his back like an old mule plowing in the field. Old mules can't work forever. The years of working in the heat, and depending on nature to feed your family, takes a toil that shows up in diseases named high blood pressure, diabetes, cancer and strokes. My daddy exchanged the plow for a broom, but his aching body forced him to retire too soon.

Caregiving taught me lessons about the pain in my daddy's body. It taught me even more about his impending death. You can't hide from death. You can run, but death is too fast to defeat in a long-distance race. For a long time, I avoided my daddy's looming death. Distance made it easy to shun images of deteriorating health. Work made it easier to escape my daddy's need for support. Running makes you weak when sickness shows up to block your escape.

Someone told me being a caregiver is an honorable decision. Many people told me I would never regret leaving Durham, North Carolina to move back home to serve my daddy. I was told it would be the hardest thing I would ever do. I was told it would be the best thing I've ever done. No one warned me to prepare for the lessons regarding limited days to discuss the long list of things never said.

There were many lessons captured in my daddy's last breath.

Some of the lessons are about life before sickness. Others are about caregiving and how it feels when you have no answers to the questions and no questions to explain the pain. The experience is both messy and rewarding. It's the hardest thing and most rewarding experience of my life.

The worst is mingled with the best. The lack of sleep and carrying the burden of not knowing enough made it the worst. Remembering how my father cleaned up my muck over the years made it the best. The best came in knowing my father deserved being cared for in a way that honored the love he showed over the years. That's the hardest lesson. It's the one about facing no more days left to say and do what's left undone.

I wish I could have done more. That's a big lesson. Learning and dealing with the guilt that comes when you wish you showed up long before aging impacts the things you want to do. The benefit of caregiving is not having to face wishing you had showed up to witness that last breath. Being present provides enough strength to exhale when it feels like you've lost your own will to breathe. Being present is not enough, but it's enough to undo a measure of guilt.

Death is a truth none of us can escape. Our parents grow older, and in time, they will need our support to make it to the end of the journey. It's easy to get trapped into believing we can escape the challenge of becoming a caregiver for our parents, but our day may come. When it does, we can only hope that others will show up to help carry the load when it's cold and you lack the strength to move beyond the wave of emotions.

I have numerous questions. I'm left wishing I knew more about my daddy's life when he lived in that raggedy house near the Missouri River. I'm left wishing I knew more about my grandparents, great-grandparents and the mighty cloud of ancestors who watch me every day. I believe they are close by, with my daddy, offering strength when the throbbing in my spirit is too much to endure alone.

3

THE OTHER HAND

My daddy's hand looked like my GI-Joe with the Kungfu grip. It was a reminder of the day my daddy accidently shot his right arm while taking aim at a rabbit. The rabbit escaped when the rifle backfired, leaving my daddy unconscious in the woods with a bleeding arm. His brothers started looking for him when he failed to come home in time for dinner.

They told me daddy almost died. He made it to the hospital in time to save his hand. The misfortune of that day in the woods cost him his talent. My aunts and uncles often talked about what could have been if not for that day in the woods. It was a high price to pay to shoot a rabbit.

I'm told my daddy was a great artist. They told me he could have attended a well-known art school in New York City, leaving life in mid-Missouri where the opportunities for black people was often limited to washing dishes, mopping floors or cleaning the houses of rich people. Going to college wasn't encouraged due to the vast limitations created by an unequal education system. My daddy could have used his art to break free from a life defined by other people's rules. His dream wasn't deferred like Langston Hughes mentioned in that poem about a raisin in the sun. My daddy's dream was abandoned when that rifle backfired in the woods.

My daddy never talked about his stiff hand. He used it to grab hold of a mop when he cleaned the floors at MFA Insurance Company. He often took me to work to eat lunch in the cafeteria. A black woman cooked the best fried chicken and I had a fancy for the apple pie with a scoop of vanilla ice cream on top. The name of the woman didn't matter as much as the assumption that cooking scrumptious chicken was the type of work black women were trained to do.

My daddy smiled with pride as people greeted us with pleasantries about how big I'd gotten since the last time I stopped by for fried chicken. Everyone stopped working and eating when daddy took me to the place where he clutched the mop with that hand that looked like my G.I Joe with the Kungfu grip.

It felt like a rite of passage in preparation of my taking hold of his broom. The smiles on the faces of the white people felt like the type of condescension that comes with the assumption that my daddy was teaching me to stay in my proper place. Those shinny floors needed attention beyond my daddy's retirement years.

My daddy's hand reflected the type of inner shame that no one talked about because it's too deep and painful to fully understand. Daddy's hand represented the myriad of shattered dreams and missed opportunities among the people who cooked for white people and kept their floors shinny.

A hand is only part of a man, but that part embodied the other parts clinging to find meaning after learning about the barriers hindering dreams. My daddy hid his pain with an infectious smile. His promise to me was more vital than the lingering pain that may have showed up when he closed his eyes at night. Maybe the pain showed up in his nightmares.

My daddy's promise to me meant more than the vanquishing of his personal dreams. He promised to feed me. He promised to provide me shelter. He promised to protect me. He promised to teach me how to be a man.

My daddy never talked about his hand. There was no talk about that day in the woods or the opportunity lost when the rabbit escaped. My daddy didn't talk about his pain with me. Maybe he had those conversations with the bottle of vodka he consumed when he was home – away from the broom and agony stirred by staying in his imposed places. Maybe the lyrics of the Blues granted him permission to consider what could have been, should have been, if not for a rifle and a rabbit in the woods.

My daddy's promise was to keep his pain to himself. These were lessons about sucking it up and acting like a man when a rifle steals your dreams. These were lessons about talking to the bottle to soothe the pain and using music to banish the demons in your head. I watched my daddy sway to the music with a glass of liquor in his left hand. I watched and learned how to survive the agony of black male disappointment.

My eyes remained glued on daddy's throbbing regret. No words. No moans. Nothing but the blues and a bottle to offer a clue regarding the voices swirling in his head.

I sat and listened as my daddy entered his escape. I was much too young to comprehend the significance of my daddy's blues. My desire to be like him kept me attached to the place where my lesson about manhood was being taught. Daddy didn't notice me. His escape from mopping floors and the part of him that stirred disappointment – his hand – were enough to keep his attention away from a little boy who wanted nothing more than to spend time with his daddy.

Watching my daddy helped fuel my love for the blues and jazz. Listening to lyrics, mingled with rhythm, began a life-long love affair with music. Like David who played the harp to ease the mental anguish of King Saul, music was my daddy's escape from the world. Like my daddy, music takes me places beyond the chaotic ways of a world that often places a proverbial foot on the neck of black men seeking to fulfill their dreams.

My daddy closed his eyes. His head titled back in a way that appeared to help the music enter his soul.

The glass gave the illusion it was glued to his left hand. The bottle of vodka rested on one of the speakers. The liquor in the bottle seemed to evaporate with the conclusion of each song. Every word seemed to touch a part that was broken.

I sat, motionless, silent, like a student taking notes. The messages in the lyrics nurtured me into the burden of manhood.

. . .

"C*AUSE* I *NEVER DID WORKIN'* *from mornin' till night*
　And my money didn't seem
　To ever come out right, no, no"
　The howl in Joe Tex's voice matched my daddy's blues.
　Papa was a tramp
　But he was a lover too
　So why can't I do like my papa do
　Alright, like papa do
　Like papa do now, 'cause I'm his son
　Why can't I be like my Daddy

T*HE* B*LUES* in my Daddy's body transferred into my soul in a way that exposed my future. Like father, like son, the questioned echoed – why can't I be like my Daddy?

With broom in hand. Smiling at white people. Talking in a way that sounded different from when he was surrounded by black people. Living in two worlds at the same time – like Paul Laurence Dunbar's poem.

We wear the mask that grins and lies,

It hides our cheeks and shades our eyes, - This debt we pay to human guile;

With tear and bleeding hearts we smile, And mouth with myriad Subtleties.

I S*AT*, learning lessons on why black people

"Wear the Mask". The lesson about black pretension. The mask of smiling faces while the heart is broken. The lesson about what it takes to make money knowing your son is watching. The lesson of pride exchanged in favor of bowing in humble submission. Lessons about why black folks shout on Sunday morning, and why liquor fills the soul like the Holy Ghost.

It felt like I was stuck there. I waited for movements to confirm he was breathing. I knew he was alive because his feet kept moving like he was playing the bass drum. When the music touched that spot – that spot between feeling the blues and the blues taking residence in your soul – daddy's head moved back and forth like he was saying no, no, no.

One day, in the middle of one of those songs, daddy noticed me. He noticed me looking at him. He noticed my admiration – at least that's what I believed. I wanted him to know I was learning about manhood. He was teaching me how to be a man. To provide for the family. To smile when in the presence of white people. To talk a certain way and make room when you saw a white person coming in your direction. I was learning about the power and message of the blues, and the peace that comes when you slowly sip liquor.

He saw me watching, and everything changed.

The look of my admiration must have exposed his shame. He quickly placed the glass next to the bottle and shifted his posture. He sat erect to evoke his lingering pride. He rubbed his head as if searching for an answer – an alternative way to teach his son lessons about manhood. He rose from his seat as if in search for a solution. The slow sips from the glass made it difficult to move in a way that reflected his mission.

He reached for the arm on the turntable and moved it to its resting place. The room became silent. The moans of the blues singers were replaced with the type of silence heard in temples just before the priest arrives to call the community to worship. It felt like a holy moment were silence and introspection serve as the liturgy for a higher form of worship.

My Daddy made his way to the closet that connected the bedroom where Sandra, Crystal I slept between mama and daddy's room. He began a search for something that would help change the narrative of a little boy learning the seduction of the blues. There were other lessons to be taught about survival when the days are made hard due to the games played to put food on the table.

He returned with a sketch pad and pencils. He placed me in the chair where he took his seat to listen to the blues. He pulled up another chair and took his seat facing me with the pad in his lap. He started drawing.

"Stay still," he said.

I noticed the pencil in his hand. He was holding it in the other hand. The left hand. Not the one that resembled my G.I. Joe with the Kungfu grip. The other one.

The frustration on his face intensified with each piece of paper he tore from the page. He struggled to get it right. The pencil seemed out of place in his left hand. Finding the right amount of pressure was difficult – too much or too little. Maybe it was the impact of the liquor in his blood. Maybe drawing my face with his left hand was too complicated.

Daddy refused to give up. I sat for over an hour. I sat for a few hours the next day, and the next, and the next. It became part of a weekend ritual – me sitting in that chair with Daddy facing me while holding a pad and pencil – in the other hand.

The frustration on Daddy's face faded as the pencil in his left hand seemed to find a home. The pieces of paper on the floor lessened, and the bottle of liquor and the sound of blues music no longer joined as part of Daddy's ritual. The inviolability in the room was the union between pad and pencil and Daddy crafting a message for his son.

The smile on his face was in stark contrast to the one I admired when I was learning lessons about the blues. Daddy bowed his head like he was praying. It felt like he was crying. I felt something moving in that space, but it was more than a seven-year-old boy could fully understand. If older, I would call it an epiphany – a divine moment that leaves you feeling like Moses, Elijah and Jesus are present to make it holy. I was too young to understand the significance of a miracle. Something beyond my Daddy empowered him to use that other hand.

It must have been my Daddy's tears that made it possible. This is what it must mean when people in the Church talk about God wiping those tears away.

My Daddy looked at me like I needed to keep taking notes. It was time for the lesson.

"Son," he began with a tone I had never heard before. "There are times in life when things happen. Something your love is taken away. You don't always get your way. When it happens. Don't ever give up. Like this hand of mine. It was taken away. Nothing I can do about it. I can't get it back."

My Daddy revealed his masterpiece - my face. He paused long enough for the lesson about manhood to penetrate my soul.

"Remember this. When the right hand don't work, the left hand will do."

It is a lesson about overcoming. It is a lesson about never giving up. It is a promise of the rewards of never giving up. It is a lesson involving using what you have when something you need is taken away. It may not look the same, but you can still recognize the picture.

I've learned to use my other hand.

4

PREPARATION

There's the move before the move. It's like the last kiss before the next kiss after saying goodbye. The next goodbye followed by another kiss with the promise it's the last kiss before the next kiss makes it harder to say goodbye. The last kiss before saying goodbye makes it harder to accept the need to walk away.

My love for Durham trapped me in a space between standing still and movement toward the unknown.

I spent two months with my father before making the final move. There was business to complete that required more than conversations on the phone. How would his bills be paid in a way that doesn't require him writing checks every month? How was he receiving his meals? His medication? His doctor appointments? The list was longer than I knew when I stepped on the plane at RDU for a two month stay in Columbia, Missouri.

As much as caregiving is about the person we love; it is also about the feelings we carry about going home. For me, leaving Columbia, Missouri was about running away. There was so much I wanted to forget – massive mistakes, feeling like less than enough, missed opportunities. My leaving was more about avoiding the drain of home. Over the years, I learned how to create a new reality devoid of the pain related to growing up with the burden of remembering me, myself and I – the three people using my name.

I recount my feelings about home in Preacha' Man, my first novel. It has taken me years to unmask the pain related to attempting to run away from what I fear the most – myself. People talk a lot about home being wherever you find yourself. It's true that home is a state of mind versus a dwelling place. That's a truth aimed at helping anyone who discovers they can't run or hide from their past.

The best way to track my thinking before deciding to become my daddy's caregiver is by revisiting my journal entries during that period. Journal writing is a vital tool for anyone interested in maintaining a discipline of self-care. It's a great way of tracking spiritual growth after long seasons of weariness.

October 12, 2012

It may help to get away. I can feel God is moving me in a different direction. I both hate and love when that happens. I love it because I'm deeply aware that I need change. I hate it because I fear what change may create. That's the sad thing about allowing yourself to be human. It comes with the type of vulnerability absent in hiding places.

I woke up thinking about the book Cecil Williams wrote – No Hiding Place. Reading it reminded me so much of my own grappling to find a place beyond pretension. It's getting harder to find that place. Why wouldn't it be hard. Reading what Williams said began a journey that made it hard for me to continue to exist within the Church. I'm not sure how I feel about that.

Is it possible to love and hate something at the same time? The obvious answer is yes. It's certain that my past relationships prove that point. I'm beginning to wonder if I'm incapable of loving what is good for me due to things lost when I step out like a blind man headed toward a cliff. You can only hope that faith creates wings just before you get to the edge.

That's what going home stirs in me. Receiving word that pops is sick has forced me to make this trip. I use the word forced

to express the fact that I don't want to go. Yes, I want to see and spend time with pops. It's the other stuff that makes it hard to go back.

I'll be there for three months. That's three months to encounter the things I've worked hard to erase from my memory.

I don't like the person Columbia created. I remain burdened by the low self-esteem and hesitation that kept me from honoring the best in me. Some of that stuff is still there, but I like to think I've grown beyond the person reared in a city that had a way of keeping black folks in their proper place.

Sadly, it took leaving to fully understand what all that means. Before leaving, I never imagined what I achieved in Durham. Yeah, I must face the fact that my radical ways have hindered some of that. If only I could keep my mouth shut and walk that thin line drawn in the sand by church folks. God knows what could have been.

It hurts coming back home as a person with far more questions than answers. I shouldn't be thinking about this. All my focus should be on pops. He needs someone there. The least I can do is stand with him during his stay in the hospital. Again. It seems to never end. In and out, in and out. I wonder if it will ever stop. I know what stopping means. I shouldn't have asked that question.

There's another question that is more perplexing. What kind of son stays away so long? My mind plays games with that question. Like an echo searching for a place to stop. Does that make sense?

Maybe not. Who knows? I suppose that's the point. None of it makes sense. No one has helped prepare me for this.

I mean, what matters the most in life? Is it craving space to be happy at the expense of the people you love? Or, is it sacrificing what makes you happy to assure your parents and other loved ones are comfortable? It feels bad choosing the first option. In many ways, it has been about me. The sad part is I've not been happy for a long time.

Why is that? Is it because everything keeps shifting, or is it because I really don't understand what it all means? I wonder if this is normal. Do other people grapple with the decision we make while pursuing happiness? I'm beginning to wonder if happiness is even a possibility.

Damn, that sounded so negative. Good thing no one is listening to what is in my head. At least I hope not. There are times when it feels like I'm walking around with a sign on my back – stay out of my way. Danger zone. This negro needs space and you don't want none of this.

No, that's not true. It may be how I feel, but I've learned the game. Play the part.

But, back to this happy thing. What is that? Maybe it's become harder due to the theology I've created to make me feel better about the confusion. That crap about God gives us joy not negated by a lack of happiness. That's what I preach and teach – a clear distinction between joy, as a fruit of the Spirit, and happiness, an emotional reaction to the human condition. Is that real or just another excuse?

See, going home is doing something that scares me. I'm afraid of that zombie feeling that pops up when I see black folk walking like death came a long time ago and they're searching for a place to cry I give up. The good news is it's only three months. The bad news is it's only three months. It's too much time for me to endure and not enough to give what pops needs.

Damn, I love that man. A part of me, most of it, wishes I was more like him. He processes the type of strength unmoved by the things that trouble me. At least that's how it appears. Maybe he's weaker than I can imagine. Why not? He's been sick for over 20 years. I can't name a sickness that he hasn't endured – cancer, diabetes, heart attack, stroke and now its meningitis. What could be next? Never mind. I hate the answer.

It's time to board this plane. Another long day on planes headed to the next mystery. I'll Holla at me later.

October 16, 2012

Where did my pops get that smile? His teeth are sickening white. It makes no sense for a person his age to smile like that with teeth worthy of a toothpaste commercial.

It's more than the smile and teeth. How does he remain so nice after all he has been through? The nurses at the rehabilitation center love him. It's not his first time there. He's a frequent flyer. They know him by name and his illnesses. How does a person live with knowing people know you by your condition?

The good news is he's closer to a release date. He misses home. Not much has changed over the years. It's the same home I knew growing up. It's amazing how much larger it seemed back then. I was so proud to live in a home owned by my father. I never endured having to pack bags due to rent not being paid or the landlord deciding to charge more for us to stay. It's the house daddy brought when I was too young to remember.

Pops told me the story about how he brought the house. He received a call from A.D. That's what he called A.D Sappington, the former president at what was MFA. It's called Shelter Insurance now.

"We were living over where they were about to build the projects," Pops said. "A.D. asked me what I was going to do when they tore everything down. I told him we would probably apply to live somewhere else."

Pops takes great pride in his stories about A.D. His pride was grounded in the white president of Columbia, Missouri's largest employer taking an interest in where he lives.

"I found a house," Pops said. "A.D. said he would meet me there. When he looked at the house, he said Carl, this house not good enough for you. You have two kids now. You need to find something better."

Pops told me he found another house and called A.D. Pops called the owner of the house and asked him to meet him to show the house to A.D.

"A.D. said this is nice. Then he asked that man how much he wanted. The man said $10,500. A.D. asked him what the $500 was for. He said it was the closing cost."

Pops laughed before telling the rest.

"A.D. wrote a check for $10,000 and told the man there won't be no closing cost," Pops said.

A.D. set up an account through the credit union. A few years later Pops received the deed to the property. He said it came just before A.D. died. There was a bond between a white man and my Pops, a custodian with the company. It was a strange friendship. Pops cut A.D.'s grass at his home across the street from Shelter Insurance. Pops drove him wherever he needed and performed other errands whenever A.D. or his wife needed.

It was a special bond that my father remembered as proof of a genuine friendship. I listened. I didn't tell him how it made me feel.

There are pictures of A.D on the wall in Pops bedroom. A.D is handing pops a plaque for 25 years of service. There's a picture in the

hallway of Pops raising the flag to begin the day at M.F.A. There's also
a grandfather clock in the front room given to Pops for serving 35
years. That's a long-time sweeping floor and running errands for your
friend.

I couldn't tell Pops how the story made me feel. I never met A.D.
He never came to our house to eat chicken or fish. I wondered if A.D.
knew my father is a great cook. My passion to cook comes from
watching Pops in the kitchen. I wonder if A.D. knew. I never shook his
hand. He didn't come to my graduation or send a card with a few
dollars tucked away in the middle. If Pops and AD were so close, why
didn't I know his friend?

I didn't tell Pops about the time I went to M.F.A to apply for a job.
They made me take a test and told me my score was too low. I left
demoralized because I had already internalized I wasn't good enough
to work alongside white people. I've wondered if the test was limited
to the black people who showed up looking for work. Back then, I
didn't consider a barrier may have been created because I'm black. It
was before I knew how to fight the power.

I couldn't say any of that. Not with that smile, laugh and an
unyielding will to see the rainbow versus the storm. God knows I wish
I was more like my daddy.

DECEMBER 2, 2012

The scars on Pops leg are getting worse. The diabetes combined
with an infection have landed him back in the hospital. The swelling
and redness make it hard for pops to maneuver around the house. Dr.
Smiley prescribed ear drops to combat the infection in his ear, but it
wasn't enough to prevent the spreading to his leg.

The trip to the doctor's offices was tough. I woke up at 6:00 a.m. To
prepare his breakfast, give him his medication, help get him dressed
and make the trip to the car in time for his appointment. It's hard
getting him in and out of the truck due to the discomfort in his leg and
the height to get into the seat.

It's cold outside and I sense pops frustration caused by not moving
fast enough. It's the first time I've encountered thoughts related to
getting older. How does a person prepare for this? How does a person

respond when the body no longer works the way it did when you're too young to imagine not being able to run and hide while playing hide and go seek or football at the Worley Street Park?

Guilt overcame me when I began pondering the energy pops has excreted in handling all this alone. My guilt was followed by anger fueled by the absence of Mama because she no longer wanted to live with Pops. The right side of my brain called it a selfish act while the left side of my brain embraced leaving as the best way to maintain sanity.

The phrase "until death do us part" took on a different meaning after I washed the urine from Pops' leg for the third time in an hour. "Until death do us part" was hard to conceive after removing soiled pants for the third time in the space of an hour. Understanding and grace transformed the resentment that blamed Mama for not being present to do what I was forced to do.

Then I gazed at the calendar that reminded me of the time left before I would return to Durham to resume my life removed from wiping waste, cooking, cleaning and making sure Pops didn't fall while making his way to the truck.

There is so much to get done before my departure. I've taken advantage of Pops time at the rehabilitation center to place his payments on automatic deduction. The thought of him writing checks and walking to the mailbox is too much. Maybe it's my way to satisfy the guilt of my leaving in 27 days. One last look at the list – electric bill, gas bill, cable, home and automobile insurance – all done. Added to the list are Mama's bills – automobile insurance and her monthly allowance. Everything will be deducted from his account. Maybe I can rest now. Maybe. No. I know it's not enough.

Pops wears a size 15 shoe. It takes time to place socks on his foot followed by the special shoes created for diabetics. He's not as big as he used to be. The neck is the same as I remember when his physique was enough to incite fear among the boys who came to the house to court Sandra. His 21-inch neck, broad shoulders and massive arms left no doubt that he was a man who succeeded in knocking people out as a boxer.

He was a Joe Frazier fan due to his politics and humble disposition. I was more "fly like a butterfly, sting like a bee" type of dude. Pops believed in staying in places white people created for black folks to exist. I was waiting for the revolution that wouldn't be televised. Gil Scott-Heron's 1971 release of the song "The Revolution Will Not Be Televised" was part of the secret world I lived in opposition to Pops' integrationist philosophy.

His body screamed fight the power, but his ways marched to the drum of white people's music. I viewed his body a waste of revolutionary potentially. As he used his strength to mop floors at Shelter Insurance, I read books by Frantz Fanon, James Baldwin and listened to recordings of speeches of Malcolm X, H. Rap Brown, Huey P. Newton and Paul Robeson.

His legs seemed swollen from years of managing white people's privilege. I can't help wondering how different things would be if Pops were given a chance to function beyond the limited space given black men when I was 15. Images of black men toting cotton and hurling large hammers on the chain gang came to mind as I washed the urine off his legs- again.

"Hey sweetie," Pops said as a nurse walked in the room to take his vitals. "You having a good day."

That smile came back like the morning sun. The sincerity of his voice did battle with the swollen, discolored leg that evokes memories of mopping and sweeping floors for minimal pay. Not much has changed since our debates on Ali versus Frazier. I'm still waiting for change to come. Pops is content with the life he's been given.

I left Columbia, Missouri two days before Christmas. I handed my daddy a hand-written letter sharing my love and respect for all he did over the years. I'm not sure if he ever read the letter. I headed back to Durham filled with guilt over leaving my daddy in a rehabilitation center. My three-month visit began an introspective journey that would result in my return the following year. I was thinking a lot about unresolved issues.

Unresolved issues are about things lost. I've learned to embrace this as a precondition to accepting the role of a caregiver. Knowing and accepting things unresolved eases the impending pain. My journal writing is a major tool in filtering through those unresolved issues. Many of my issues were buried beneath layers of survival skills.

Others demanded attention based on how they showed up as dysfunctional patterns.

My journal writing challenged me to structure my feelings related to loss. Some feelings are characterized as my personal loss stirred by my becoming a caregiver – the loss of familiar space, the loss of friends, the loss of career. Other feelings conveyed thoughts surrounding witnessing the loss my father endured – his heath, aging, the inability to manage responsibilities.

Reflecting on loss demands a willingness to view transition as movement toward gain. In doing so, my feelings involving loss required more than a summation of the things I sacrificed to become a caregiver. It is critical to observe loss as progress toward overcoming unresolved issues. Becoming a caregiver is a decision aimed at stimulating affirmative change.

5

HOME AS THE CONDUIT FOR CHANGE

There's that moment when you know you must go home. Getting there isn't easy. For me, it came after a long season of stripping. Little by little, things were taken away in a way that left me believing God was trying to get my attention. Doing the right thing becomes complicated when we are enamored with things - things like work, friends, lovers and material - things.

This was the death before the death. The call intensified the pain of my lingering emotional death.

My mama called to tell me a neighbor found my daddy naked on the bathroom floor. He was found in a diabetic coma. It wasn't the first time. My daddy lived alone after Mama left him to take care of her brother and sister-in-law two hours away from where my daddy lived. My sister was also two hours away. My daddy had a nephew who checked in from time to time.

Daddy is home alone, I thought as Mama gave the details. He might not make it. This could be the end. He was naked because he was trying to get to the bathroom before it was too late. He struggled to get there. He fell. It was too hard. He needed help. Daddy is alone. There is no one there. Why is Daddy alone? I'm here. He's there. My daddy needs me.

Thoughts before what felt like impending death.

Everything was falling apart. I prayed.

The stripping of things wasn't enough to make the decision easy. Faith pressed my desire to stay. I knew my death was for a season – joy would come in the morning. My weeping was only for a night. I prayed all night.

"Take this cup from me, Lord," mine was a prayer like Jesus' in the Garden of Gethsemane. That's how it felt. "Don't make me drink from this cup. I can't go back home."

I pleaded with God to find another way. Not me, Lord. Please, not me. I prayed until it felt like blood was seeping from a vein on my forehead. I prayed until my body ached from the force of my tears. I prayed until the setting of the sun shifted to the despair of midnight.

I did more begging than praying. I didn't want to go home. I feared home. I agonized over the loss of my life even though it felt like death. Death in Durham seemed better than life in Columbia, Missouri. I prayed and prayed. I cried and cried.

My pleading didn't change the answer. I knew I had to go home. It hurt. I dreaded the answer. I heard the maddening voices announce, "ashes to ashes, dust to dust." I felt my own death coming with the decision to go home. I couldn't say no. I had to go. I knew it the moment my mother told me my father was found naked in a coma on the bathroom floor.

Home was the place of my greatest disappointments. It's where I used drugs to cover the pain of Crystal's death. Crystal, my baby sister, died shortly after turning 13 after a long battle with brain cancer. After she died, I used drugs to numb the pain. Living in Columbia, Missouri felt like a reason to give up hope. I assumed being black was a life sentence to never being good enough.

Home was a reminder of economic disparity and doors rarely opening no matter how hard I prayed. I feared going back. I begged God not to do it – don't make me go back.

I had to go.

Acceptance changes everything. It happened when I noticed the sun rising. The tears stopped. I stopped fighting. I let go of the fear and accepted I had to go back home. In what seemed like seconds, I transitioned from fighting to planning. It was time to leave Durham.

I let go of the pain related to the things I would miss – my friends, my favorite coffee house, all of the great places to eat, Duke Gardens, concerts at the Carolina Theatre, plays at the Durham Performance Arts Center, art at the Nasher Museum, The American Dance Festival, my Saturday morning breakfast club – there was so much I would miss.

Within those seconds, I began planning to give what remained away. There were things I couldn't take with me. I gave away furniture, artwork, music, books and other things obtained over the years. I placed the rest in storage in a friend's attic. I gave away a car but held onto a bunch of memories. I contacted my editor at the Durham News to inform him I was leaving. He asked when, I told him within 30 days.

I purchased a ticket. Wrote a farewell column, contacted all my friends and planned a farewell party at the Beyu Café. The clock was ticking on going back home. My children were glad to know Grandpa wouldn't be alone. I told Daddy I would be there soon. He was healing at a rehabilitation center. Mama was overjoyed and Sandra, my sister, looked forward to seeing her little brother come back home.

I packed some clothes and left the rest with another friend. She would ship them after I arrived. The days rapidly approached for my departure. The hardest part was behind me – saying goodbye to all my friends. The newspaper printed an article about my leaving. After all those sermons and columns, I was told a part of the city's heart was leaving. It was hard to imagine what life would be like without Durham.

Twenty-five years had passed since I arrived in Durham to study at Duke Divinity School. I'd met many people and made my share of critics. I raised my children, made numerous mistakes and learned tough lessons.

The decision to leave was the hardest part. That's the part I had to make alone. The steps after deciding were easy. I never felt I was making those steps alone. I was carried by forces behind my will to move. Numerous people encouraged me with their own stories of caregiving. They told me it was the hardest thing they ever did. They told me it would change me. They told me they were glad they did it and it is the best decision they ever made.

The messengers came from all directions – at coffeehouses, grocery stores, while eating, while walking, while sitting on a bus or reading a book – people told me their stories about caregiving. They represented all races, religions, men and women, younger and older than me. Caregiving seemed to touch most of them in the same way. It didn't matter how they felt about the person they cared for before making the decision. Some of them had fond memories before making the decision. Some of them had issues with the person that went unresolved before death. Some talked about getting closer, while others talked about resolving issues from long ago.

Caregiving has cleansing powers. It's grueling.

It's painful. It's complicated.

I was told all of that before getting on the plane. I heard all of it, but none of it prepared me for what I experienced when I arrived to take care of my daddy.

What is it about going home that makes it so hard to go? It's not the place. It's what we want to forget. It's what we left behind. It's the part of our identity rejected when we left. Leaving home offers the opportunity to recreate ourselves. We write a new story unlike the one we left behind. Home is bursting with people who know the truth lost in the narrative created after you walked away.

Returning home is a conduit for channeling change by forcing an examination of the total self. Home eliminates the ability to create an alternative conclusion. The error in returning home is the denial of the truth fostered by experiences after leaving home. We are more than the parts measured by space and time. We are the totality of encounters and relationships that form our wholistic identity. Returning home forced the merging of separate identities created in the places I called home.

Returning home defied the characterization of my former self. Rather than walking and speaking based on the terms of my former identity, I brought a new awareness of my place in the world and new language to characterize my individuality. Returning home forced an embrace of the person who once walked in the same spaces, while celebrating a will to overcome the sense of brokenness provoked during my earlier years. Returning home fortified my perception of the new me inspired by the lessons of the old me.

Returning home gave me permission to re-introduce myself to my daddy and other family members. They knew and loved the person who left long ago, but barely knew the man who changed for better and, in many cases, for worse. Caregiving evoked my will to face my need to confront myself. This is a critical benefit to caregiving that is often lost in the pursuit of daily survival.

6

GETTING TO KNOW ME

Flight 1972 departed Raleigh/Durham on Saturday, October 5, 2013. I arrived in Charlotte at 1:52 p.m. before boarding flight 1801 to St. Louis at 2:47 p.m. I landed in St. Louis at 3:34 p.m. I sat on the 19th row, seat D. The details are fastened in my memory.

It was cold when I landed. My friend Deborah was waiting for me at the airport. Her warm smile helped me endure the cold. It's cold in Missouri, a fact I'd forgotten since my long stay in North Carolina. We know cold in the South, but Missouri cold is a different type of cold. It bruises the body and your spit freezes before it hits the ground. The ride back home gave me a chance to ponder my decision.

Deborah was the perfect bridge between life in North Carolina and my decision to come back home. It helped knowing I had a friend less than two hours away to help me withstand the lonely days. I wasn't alone, but there wasn't much to match what I left behind. I made a mental list of old friends and family members. I wondered who still lived in Columbia. I wondered who would remember me. It was a short list.

Deborah and I talked about music, the work of the church and my decision. She shared her thoughts regarding the death of her father, and how she often struggled to make it through the days. It was the same story I'd heard from others. The pain caused by the loss seem-

ingly never goes away. There are so many memories. Like me, her faith
and work at a church helped overcome some of the pain. The conversation confirmed my decision. Coming home was the right thing to do. It
would be the hardest thing I've ever done. It would be the most
rewarding experience of my life.

I'd heard it enough to believe it's true

Daddy was waiting for my arrival. He was in better health than I
assumed. He was home alone after spending more than 60 days
between the hospital and a rehabilitation center. He was glad to see
me. His joyful disposition after meeting Deborah left him conjuring
thoughts about the nature of our friendship. Just friends. Really, we're
just friends. Daddy's infectious smile reflected his desire for me. It
would be better if I had a girlfriend. It would help knowing I wouldn't
have to spend my time taking care of him. Maybe Daddy knew what
was coming – days of extreme loneliness packed in between cooking
meals, taking vital signs, giving him medication, washing clothes and
helping him get to and from his truck for doctor appointments.

I took my luggage to the bedroom once shared by Crystal and
Sandra. I reflected on the days before Daddy remolded the house to
add an additional bedroom, family room and storage space. My old
bedroom was converted into a sewing room shortly after I left home
to attend college. That room was packed with old newspaper articles,
books and photo albums. It was the space left to collect family memories. Memories of my mama remained to solidify her continued role
as the matriarch of the family. The love between my daddy and
mama didn't change when she moved to Waynesville, Missouri to
take care of my uncle Loucious. She stayed after my uncle and his
wife both died. Her stuff remained as a reminder of her continued
presence.

My daddy and mama had a complicated marriage held together by
countless memories. Every day, my daddy would ask me about
my mama.

"You talk to your mother today," he said. I would answer yes or no.

"She need anything? Send her some."

It happened everyday after taking his vitals. "She probably needs
something."

My daddy was quick to remind me of his commitment.

"When I promised God to love your mama until I die, I meant it," he said. "It don't matter if she's here. She will always be my wife."

My mama's spirit was still in the house. Her clothes hung in the closet where I placed my bags. Her clothes and shoes were in each bedroom – all three – to display her place in my daddy's heart. I gazed over the clothes packed in the closet. There was no space for mine. I exhaled knowing the rest of my wardrobe would be shipped from Durham later. I decided to leave it for another day.

I returned to the living room to interrupt the conversation between Deborah and my daddy. It felt like love at first sight. Daddy's charm had heightened over time. His way with words reminded me of where I got it from. Like father, like son. I shared in the conversation long enough to remind them I was still there. I then departed to the kitchen to evaluate the items in the refrigerator. The first thing I noticed was the insulin medication. There were two types – some in a bottle that required needles, and the type that resembled a large magic marker with a dial on the end. There was enough to last two weeks. I checked the expiration dates. We were in good shape.

I opened the freezer and was overwhelmed by stacks of meals that reminded me of TV dinners. Most of them appeared to be freezer burned. I couldn't tell how long they had been there, but I knew they predated his recent stay in the hospital and rehabilitation center. The thought of how they tasted made me sick. I was thankful my daddy had food prepared for him by volunteers at Meals on Wheels, but I couldn't help believing it's not good enough for my daddy. My daddy deserved better than this.

I begged God for forgiveness for thinking my daddy was too good for the meals stacked in his freezer. I pondered the time I spent at the Meals on Wheels office in Durham. I thought of my service as President of Durham Congregations in Actions, the interfaith, interracial religious coalition that helped start Meals on Wheels and the other agencies at the Urban Ministries building. I had no problem affirming the importance of these ministries for others, but I couldn't fathom my daddy being relegated to depending on these meals. My privilege was showing.

I decided to cook for my daddy – breakfast, lunch and dinner. I would cook nutritious meals that considered his health concerns.

Daddy was a diabetic. His blood pressure never presented a problem, but I considered the possibility. I prepared a list of items to purchase at the grocery store. My daddy would eat like a king. Why not? My daddy is a king.

I opened the door beside the refrigerator and took the two steps down to enter the garage. It was chilly. The washing machine and dryer seemed to be in working condition. I remembered when daddy purchased the set from Sears when I was in high school. Like everything else in the house, they withered the test of time. The furniture in the living room was purchased when I was in elementary school. When the fabric went bad, daddy had the couch and chair reupholstered. He did so after a lecture about buying good stuff because it will last longer than the cheap stuff young folks buy.

The furniture in the family room was purchased when I was in middle school. The furniture in the bedrooms were purchased when my daddy and his friends built the addition to the house. Not much had changed other than a few stains on the carpet Daddy installed when he got tired of taking care of the hardwood floors.

It was cold in the garage. Daddy installed a heater after I left to go to college. It didn't work.

Washing clothes in the Winter would be hard to endure. I thought about how Daddy kept his clothes clean given the two steps down to enter the garage and the chill in the Winter. I decided to wash clothes twice a week – on Tuesday and Thursday – to keep the load small. My plan became comical once Daddy became too sick to control the yuck in his belly.

I noticed a makeshift closet in the garage. Daddy built it to provide additional space for Mama's wardrobe. Mama used to make her own clothes along with those fancy hats she wore on Sunday's to maintain the tradition of the Mothers of the Church displaying their crowns. Mama was a seamstress who once made a living designing and making robes for clergy. The closet in the garage was like the others in the house – packed with memories of Mama's presence. I closed the door and headed back in the house to continue my assessment.

The linen closet between my old and new bedrooms was stacked with boxes of insulin syringes, test strips, lancing devices and glucose meters. A few bath towels and linens were there, but the bulk of the space was consumed with enough supplies to last more than a year. Most of the space in the drawer chest in my new room was crammed with more supplies. The same applied to the closet in my old bedroom. The house was overflowing with medical supplies.

I soon discovered the game played by companies willing to take advantage of senior citizens with medical insurance and Medicare. They called once a month to inform customers of the need for a new shipment. They never stopped to ask if they needed more. My daddy would always accept the offer. I wonder how much of taxpayer's money is spent on medical supplies that is never used. The salespeople on the other end of the call seemed shocked when I informed them not to call us, we'll call them.

A quick scan of my daddy's house shocked me into my new reality. It was cold in my new room, and daddy like things hot – real hot. Aging, combined with his diabetes, made it hard for him to stay warm. The thermostat stayed on 77 degrees, but it wasn't enough to alter the temperature on my side of the house. I went to bed with layers of pajamas and a space heater near the bed to make me more comfortable at night. The space was much smaller than my former bedroom in Durham. My master suite was exchanged for a room designed for two girls under the age of 15. The furniture was matching twin beds and a white dresser.

Nothing in the room had changed other than the small desk my mother placed in the room to create more space for her knick-knacks that once lived in my former bedroom. The wine-colored carpet was long past need of being replaced, and the windows were glued shut to prevent people from opening them when there was need for air. The wallpaper in the room reminded me of the interior design trends from the early 70's. My new home was an extreme departure from my bachelor pad back in West Village – the old tobacco warehouse converted into loft apartments. I took a few moments to reminisce on downtown living with high ceilings, wood floors and the brick walls aimed at mimicking space somewhere in New York City.

The decision to move back home was an ongoing reminder of what used to be before Daddy needed me to come back home. My tour of my new – former -dwelling place stirred memories from my childhood. Although it was just space, this space represented the things I vowed to leave behind once I was old enough to decide on the lifestyle that reflected my personal taste. This space exposed the deep contradiction between myself and my daddy. More than a case of difference related to interior design, this new space uncovered our divergent views regarding what matters and why.

My decision to move back home to take care of my daddy forced me to embrace the space I fought to leave behind. My love for cooking would be done in an outdated kitchen. My clothes would be stored in a closet designed for girls. My queen-sized bed with silk linens were replaced with old linens that didn't match. Those high ceiling were gone. I would sleep in a room with wallpaper with flowers adjacent to a room with wood paneling. My CD's were stored in Durham along with my books. Most of my art was given away along with the numerous mementoes that brought me joy when I needed a fond memory.

In that moment, I seemed trapped in things lost. I allowed myself to feel all of it – the woman who I loved was left behind. The place I prayed would be our home was gone. My friends who made my life complete and the places I loved to stir my foodie cravings, all of it was far away. I was back in the place I left behind. I was back in the place of older memories, some of which I wanted to leave behind to create a new reality.

I stood in the middle of the room my daddy built in the early 70's. The paneled walls in the family room were covered with pictures from a different time. I gazed at the picture of a skinner me grabbing my high school diploma. There was the picture of me in a sleeveless shirt and bald head. An earring dangled from my left ear. It was the picture that appeared in the Columbia Daily Tribune to report my selection as a representative to Missouri's Boy's State. Back then I had no clue regarding how prestigious it was to be selected.

"I could have worn a suit and tie," I giggled as I pondered how immature I was back then.

I scanned the other pictures – the cute one of King, Lenise and Krista, my three children, when they were all under the age of 10. All three were smiling. I missed my kids. There were pictures of Kathy, my former wife, Andre, my nephew, Sharhonda, my niece and Sandra, my sister. I noted the pictures of Mama and Daddy during times before I left Columbia to create my new version of reality. Then I saw the picture that forced the tears.

It was the picture of Crystal before she got sick. She was 12 years-old when the picture was taken. It was taken before she lost her hair from the chemotherapy treatment. It was taken before she lost her ability to walk without the support of a walker. The picture was placed on the wall where the bed was placed before she died. I stood near the place where she laid in a comma before taking her last breath. The same place where it felt like my heart stopped beating before running to my old bedroom to curse God.

I asked God why not me? Why did she have to die instead of me? I deserved to die. She deserved to live.

My standing near the same place took on new meaning. Coming home, in that instant, made it clear why it was hard to make the decision to come back home. I was there to revisit death. I was there to recall the reasons I refused to come home. There were mounds of pain I refused to consider. I was back to revisit death – the death of Crystal and the impending death of my father. All of that was clear, but I was back home to ponder my own death – the death covered by the rhetoric of my religion. The death of my soul when Crystal died that day. The death that came with my quest to hide behind the good news that failed to take the pain away. A part of me died a long time ago, and I was back home to face the burden of my own death.

My decision to come home was about taking care of my daddy, but it was also about my daddy taking care of me.

It's Cold isn't Just About the Weather

"The best way to start is to say I have no life outside of my dad. It's rare that I find time to explore anything else. It feels like I have opted to give all of me to him. There is no help – no family, no friends – willing to support me in this. I'm already tired; need hugs and a real conversation," I wrote in an email on October 21, 2013.

"My personal battles are legion – from the boxes of clothes left in Durham, to a lack of space for me, to no friends, no love life and no work. On top of that, I wonder how work is possible given his current state." Lorna, a member of my Saturday Morning Breakfast Club understood. Like me, she was entangled in taking care of a parent. My email vent was what I needed to remember it's not just me. There are others – like a legion – grappling with balancing caregiving with the desire for work, play, love and finding space to breathe.

It only took me 16 days to feel the burden. Between cooking, washing dishes without the convenience of a dishwasher, washing clothes, and on and on, there was no time or energy to ponder ways to balance my days. My typical day started at 7:00 a.m., but that depended on the circumstance of the night.

Sleeping was complicated by the fear. I feared a fall or the call of my name to help Daddy make it to the bathroom. It took only 16 days for me to name what Daddy did a miracle. How did he do it alone? How did he find the strength to make it to the bathroom without the support of another person?

It was a miracle.

Sleeping was complicated by the cold. My bones ached, and it felt like what I've read about frostbite. It had to be the coldest day ever. The sound of the wind combined with the mounting snow made it impossible for me to envision going outside. My skin resembled crusty leather and my desire to urinate was interrupted by thoughts of the cold outside the layers of clothes and blankets.

Then I heard the moans. It was my daddy's plea just before his guts exploded to release his breakfast, lunch and dinner. He didn't call my name. Not this time. The moan was enough to shift my attention from the cold to rescue Daddy before it was too late. I arrived by Daddy's bedside to witness him struggling to maneuver his walker to make the trip to the bathroom not far away. It wasn't far, maybe 20 – 25 steps, but it's a long way when one's strength has faded due to aging and a sickness that refused to go away.

Watching Daddy battle the walker for position recapped previous thoughts. It's a miracle. How did Daddy do this – alone.

I rushed to his side fearing another fall. Daddy was heavy. Although much smaller than when I was younger, it was easy to conjure thoughts of a man known to be a great boxer. His 21-inch neck, size 15 shoes and massive chest made it complicated for one person to lift him after a fall. It's a point I learned after frequent trips to the bedroom to pick him up from the floor. It reminded me of lifting weights – bend your knees, keep your back straight, use your legs versus depending on your arm strength – all these lessons came back.

It's harder lifting weights when you're over 50.

I need to join a gym. I'm too old for this. I can't do this alone. How did Daddy do this, all came to mind with every failed attempt to lift Daddy from the floor. I prayed he wouldn't fall.

Too late.

I felt like I pulled every muscle in my body. Daddy's inability to contribute in my effort to get him back on the bad left me frustrated. After what seemed like forever of grabbing him, pulling him, bending knees, pausing to rest, praying and giving up – I finally got him on the bed. I was able to get enough of his back on the edge. From there, I picked him up and placed him on the bed.

Daddy was wet.

The look on his face reminded me of my need not to show my frustration. His eyes told the story of a man aggravated by an inability to take care of himself.

"It's okay," I whispered. I could tell Daddy wanted to cry. Maybe there were tears I couldn't see. I thought of how I would feel if in his position. How would I feel if my son changed my clothes after peeing on myself? How would I feel if my son had to help me get off the floor because I lacked the strength? How would I feel if my body was too weak to do things, I once took for granted?

I dashed to the bathroom after grabbing a washcloth. After waiting for the water from the sink to turn warm, I filled the yellow wash bucket with water and squirted enough body wash to form bubbles. The sound of Daddy's moans from the bedroom across the hall served as a clock counting down the time needed to rush back.

I hurried back and placed the wash clothes inside the bucket. There was no space on the nightstand near the bed to place the bucket. That space was occupied by the telephone, television remote and blood pressure monitor attached to his telephone. Every morning, at nine-o'clock, the phone rang with a command to attach the blood pressure cuff to his arm and oxygen sensor to his index finger. The levels were transmitted to his home healthcare company through the phone. It was a system that came with ongoing harassment from a nurse over the phone if the process failed to be completed. I appreciated the pestering.

I placed the bucket on the dresser near the wall across from the bed. An old office chair was placed near Grandma's old clothes chest. It was painted white, hiding the oak and finish that made it a valued piece of furniture before aging and neglect hid its glory. Thoughts of how the chest reminded me of my daddy – a great man succumbing to the impact of decades of neglect.

The old office chair was moved from my Mama's sewing room – my former bedroom – for family members and home health nurses to sit when taking care of my daddy. I placed the stack of towels on the top of the chest on the chair. I placed one of the towels on the bed, next to where my daddy was sitting.

I quickly, but gently, removed the gray sweatpants off my daddy. His legs were sore from the impact of diabetes. The wounds on his legs, ankles and feet required the care of both a wound specialist and home healthcare nurse. Every week, I placed daddy in his Ford F-150 truck to make the trip to the doctor's office across from Boone County Hospital. It wasn't a long trip, but it seemed like forever due to the complications involved in getting daddy dressed and into the truck when it's cold outside and the ground is covered with ice and snow.

I unwrapped the bandage from his right leg. The wounds were worse. I did my best to wipe the urine off his legs. His normal dark skin was replaced by a tone of red. From his calf to his ankle, his skin was shedding and the red of his flesh was creeping up his leg. The swelling of his toes exposed the weakness of enduring the impurity in his body. I did my best to wipe the illness away.

Daddy looked at me. Something was different. I could see it in his eyes. It was worse than before. My lack of training hid the truth glaring at me. There was a new type of sickness assaulting my daddy's body. His face was speaking, but my desire to wash it away, like the sins before baptism, kept me from seeing and hearing the truth. His eyes were crying. His body was screaming.

I wiped daddy's legs and covered his wounds with fresh bandages. I concealed his oozing flesh with white bandages like the Church hides the sins of the powerful in the presence of the weak. I placed dry sweatpants on my daddy's body. I pulled the pants from the stack in the top drawer in the dresser across from my daddy's bed. After taking the soggy pants off, I placed the clean pants on gently. I treated my daddy's body like the temple of the Holy Ghost. It was a sacred moment that needed a benediction.

The floodgate opened. More urine flowed down his leg.

He looked at me – more perplexed than before. I could hear daddy's heart speak, I'm sorry. I couldn't stop it. I tried…

"It's okay daddy," I grabbed his sweatpants and pulled them off, just like before.

It was easier this time. The wash bucket was near. The water was still warm. The urine didn't soak the fresh bandage. I grabbed the green sweatpants and placed the gray pants on top of the other soaked pants in the clothes basked next to my chair. I looked at the clean stack of sweatpants in the drawer – only two left. Four dirty sweatpants in the basket roused the need for me to wash clothes.

I snatched the clothes basket as soon as I covered Daddy with the blankets on the bed and another in the clothes chest. It was cold. I rushed through the house to make my way to the washing machine in the garage. I turned on the lights in the kitchens before making my way to the door between the refrigerator and stove. Once there, I turned on the light in the garage and made my way down the two steps leading to the garage. The concrete steps matched the floor in the garage. I was cold. My white athletic socks and linen pajamas weren't enough to bear the cold.

"It won't take long," I murmured while placing the clothes in the washing machine. I placed enough detergent on top and selected warm water and medium load.

"I did it again," my daddy screamed as I closed the washing machine. "I did it again."

I hurried my pace, walking as fast as my chilly feet and hands allowed. I almost fell as I took the first step up the stairs – another reminder of the miracle. How did Daddy do it? Once inside, I raced through the kitchen, made the quick right turn through the living room and sharp left turn into the bedroom. Daddy was sitting on the side of the bed waiting for my return.

I removed his wet sweatpants, again. I wiped the urine off his legs, again. I grabbed clean sweatpants from the drawer, again, and put them over his ailing feet and legs. I gently placed the large socks back on his feet, again, and helped him back in bed. I covered him with the blankets while watching my daddy fight back the tears.

"This is probably harder for him than it is for me," I thought as I did my best to convince my daddy everything would be alright.

I took hold of the urine stained sweatpants and hurried back to the garage to add them to the load before the machine started to spin. The bite of the cold seemed less due to the back and forth journey between the bedroom and garage. The warmth failed to lessen the weariness caused by lack of sleep. I reached for the lid in time to give the murky addition time to soak.

My right foot slipped as I reached for the lid. My right hand slammed against the rubber pipe connected to the hose. Water burst against my chest with a vicious force that drenched my chest with chilled water. I felt the cold on the other side of the garage walls. I felt the force of the wind. I felt the burden of a cold too harsh to withstand. My glasses were saturated with water. It felt like the chill would create a layer of ice making it impossible to see. My hair felt like icicles on a tree. The water dripped from my hair to my chest, from my chest all the way down my feet.

I reached for the pipes attempting to attach the pipe back on the hose. The force of the water was too much to make it fit. My hands felt like the early stage of frost bite, but I was able to turn the water off. Maybe I can fix it, I imagined as I looked for a wrench or anything to transform me into an amateur plumber. I wiped the water from my glasses to help me see the task I faced.

It was worse than I assumed. It wasn't the force of my stumbling that caused the detachment of the pipe. The pipe burst due to the cold temperature. I stood with no solution. I lacked the knowledge.

"Carl Jr.," I heard the voice of my daddy from the bedroom. "I did it again."

He did it again. Only one clean sweatpants remained. The others soaked in the cold water, and I lacked the knowledge needed to fix the washing machine. I stood immobilized. Drenched in cold water with a body sapped by the toil of the night, I lacked the will to move. I lacked the hope and strength to take another step.

I cried. Not for myself, but for my daddy. I felt the pain of failure. He needed what I was incapable of giving.

"Carl Jr.," his voice sounded like a prayer. My daddy's voice mingled with my tears until the answer came to me.

I prayed.

"Fix it lord," my body trembled. I wasn't sure if it was the cold or the fear. Maybe it was the combination of both. I prayed. "Fix it Lord."

The prayer worked. I moved, one step after another. Slow at first. The pace intensified as the sound of my daddy's voice seemed to echo in my head.

"Carl Jr.," his voice was weak. It sounded like he felt I must have left him alone. Alone. Alone like before when he was found on the bathroom floor. Alone. Alone like so many other days when my daddy was forced to find the strength to change his clothes – alone.

"I'm here Daddy," I cried, hoping my prayer for peace camouflaged my fear. "I'm here Daddy."

I gently removed his sweatpants, again. I wiped the urine from his body and replaced the sodden bandages from his leg and foot. I placed the gold sweatpants – the last clean sweatpants – over his ailing foot, ankle ad leg. Again. I lifted him to slip the sweatpants over his legs and buttocks, again. I helped my daddy lay down and placed the blankets over him. I prayed as I took care of my daddy. I prayed while fighting back the tears.

I placed two pillows under his head and helped him turn on his left side. Once Daddy was comfortable, I reached for one of the towels on the dresser across from his bed. I wiped the cold water mixed with my tears off my face. I wiped the cold water off my chest, stomach and feet. Then I paused waiting for what would come next. I waited for the impossible to arrive – no more clean sweatpants.

I took a seat in the old office chair near my daddy's bed. I waited. I prayed. Then it happened.

Daddy was snoring.

My prayer was answered.

That night changed me. The memory of cold water gushing against my chest shapes the way I think about life, love and faith. There are few recollections that come close to conjuring the fear of that moment. Experiencing the chill of water spurting all over me, shifted the way I think about what it means to experience life grounded by a constant faith. My faith was challenged that night. In being confronted by the assumptions of my faith, my faith intensified that night.

My moment of weakness reinforced what I've always known to be true. There are considerable limitations that we all are forced to concede. There are things none of us can fix – not with our prayers, trust or potential. That night, I found myself burdened by my frailty. I was too weak to fix it. I was cold, tired, frustrated, afraid and vastly unskilled. I'm not a nurse. I'm not a plumber. I'm not trained in how to lift a 250-pound man from a floor unto a bed.

There are the natural limits that come with aging. That night forced me to consider my own mortality. Yes, like my daddy, my day will come soon. What will my life be like when I'm incapable of changing my clothes after urinating on myself? What will I feel when I'm too weak to walk to the bathroom alone, and my legs lack the strength to maintain balance? Who will be there for me when I scream for help? Will I be alone like my daddy before I made the decision to come home?

As much as that night was about my relationship with my daddy, it also exposed my personal fears. In that moment of reflection, I was pried into contemplating meanings beyond the obvious. It's obvious my daddy needed the love and care of his son, but there was more to consider. This was about daddy's need, but is was also about my own needs – both in that moment and in days to come. My being present with my daddy triggered the fear that no one would be there for me.

This was a moment to ponder all the things taken for granted. Have I taken my children for granted? Have I done enough in loving them to secure their support when my time for caregiving approaches? If not, have I taken for granted the resources needed to assure a place to live when I lack the strength to move? Have I invested enough to make it possible to survive beyond my productive years? If not, what will become of me?

That night exposed the frailty of life. My daddy taught me numerous lessons about preparing for tomorrow. He told me to save money, not to waste what you make on nonessential thrills and to make provisions for your children. My daddy's life was an example of sacrifice. His entire life was dedicated to taking care of his wife and children. He saved money for those rainy days. Would I have enough to do the same?

That night pressed deeper internal deliberation regarding my daddy's assumptions. Was it all worth it? My mama was no longer there. The stress of caregiving was too much for her to endure. My older sister was not there. She was over 100 miles away grappling to make those ends meet. My daddy's allegiance in providing for his wife and children was not enough to assure our presence when he needed us the most.

Did I come home too late?

My daddy gave all he could a satisfy the needs of his family. His wardrobe consisted of sweat suits, the socks he obtained from hospital visits, three pairs of shoes and two winter coats. Daddy got rid of the suits, shirts and ties after he retired from the upgraded job he obtained at Shelter Insurance Company. After all those years of sweeping and mopping floors, my daddy moved into a management position. He gave orders to the men and women who performed the job he maintained for over 25 years. Daddy ditched his newfound work attire and replaced them with those sweat suits.

His wardrobe depicted his commitments. The first color television he purchased in 1965 remains in the living room. It serves as a piece of furniture with family pictures, an antique Kerosene lamp and a plant on top. His bedroom is a tribute to the 1980's with an outdated post bed and matching furniture that continues to be my daddy's pride. The mattress is the same he purchased with the bedroom furniture. Everything in the house displays decades before the new millennium.

My daddy is the model of simplicity

"All I ever wanted was to provide for my wife and children and to buy a truck," my daddy would say to declare his life purpose.

Unlike his brothers and nephews, my daddy didn't spend money on fast cars and name brand clothes. My daddy never gambled his money away like other men in our family. There weren't any women with their hands out for money to pay child support or to coverup an extramarital affair. Daddy's money went to support his wife and children. That and the black Ford F-150 parked in front of the house.

That was the lesson my daddy taught me. Watching my daddy tussle with himself pressed me into considering the meaning of it all. Was it worth it? My daddy's lesson was about the later years, but does it matter when you are alone with no family to honor the sacrifices made to support them?

It's the common question I ask whenever I make a visit to a rehabilitation center. It's not my right to judge families for placing a person in a rehabilitation facility. Caregiving is a grueling task that leaves those engaged worse off than many imagine. It requires a level of strain that makes it difficult to maintain the strength necessary to offset the burden. Sadly, most caregivers are left broken long after the death of the person they serve.

But that question remains, what goes into a family member making that decision? My long chilly night provided an answer to that question. They do it because it's too much for one person to handle alone. Knowing that isn't enough to offset the pain related to making that decision. Nothing can soothe that angst.

Nothing. Not time after it's all over. Not nice words placed in wishing you well cards or flowers to express sadness. No matter what decision families make – caregiving versus a rehabilitation center – the deep anxiety doesn't fade.

7

THE DEATH WISH

There are some relatives who discard family members like old clothes taken to a Goodwill thrift store for a tax deduction. No matter how much you give, it never seems to be enough. It's not enough due to the vast limitations we bring to our effort of caregiving.

My daddy is worth more than old clothes. That's not to say I never thought about gaining independence before he died. Preparing for my daddy's death taught me the limits of dreams. My daddy's sickness and death forced questions regarding the meaning of my life. I was challenged by the desire to ask the question "what about me?"

What does it profit a person to gain the benefit of caregiving while losing their dreams? By dreams I mean basic things. Things like the freedom to explore life without the burden of taking care of a person. Things like not feeling guilty for desiring more than the pleasure of being present.

Caregiving cultivates guilt in wishing your family member would die. It's easy to justify these feelings based on the pain we witness. Death must be better than this. Daddy would be better off if he died to spend his afterlife with Jesus. It's easy to use faith in streets paved with gold to counterbalance the wish to be set free from the burden of caregiving.

I call this the "death wish".

The death wish is normal reaction. Rather than exposing the weakness of caregivers, it reflects the humanity of caregiving. It bares the vast limitations of giving and the effects of deprived balance. The death wish is not a prayer for a family member to die. It's a plea for the caregiver to live.

My desire to learn more about my daddy helped me neutralize the death wish. I contemplated the massive limits my daddy faced throughout his life. What is the deeper meaning of hard work to provide for his family? What does it mean to give so much for others while receiving so little in return? My questions forced a critique regarding my assumptions involving what it means to be a man. I was taught to work hard, take care of myself and prepare for my last days.

My daddy's life and lessons stirred me away from the death wish. My wish seemed selfish in the face of all my daddy did for me, my mama and my sisters. I felt guilty for wishing my daddy would die to set me free. It was easy to condemn my wish for the agony of caregiving to go away. I kept these thoughts to myself. They seemed cruel. I unraveled my thoughts as egotistical prompts of all I have taken for granted.

It's critical that caregivers embrace the death wish as a sign of something missing. It's a natural warning regarding the loss of independence. Caregiving uncovers extreme changes in the life of a family member. No matter how hard we try, no matter how much we learn – the time will come when you still need help after peeing on yourself. Caregiving teaches lessons regarding the limits of self-sufficiency, the agony of aging and death.

In addition to what we learn through witnessing the decline of another person, caregiving exposes the limits of giving. Our bodies are fragile. Our emotions are delicate when self-care is abandoned. Hope for the future is obstructed by the constant toil of caregiving - washing the urine and muck, placing Daddy on the toilet, carrying Daddy to bed his and placing a blanket on his body before turning the light off and saying goodnight.

Caregiving is a reminder of the limits of giving when faced with the reality of your own declining health. Soon, you will need support. Everything fades. The money, the moments of solitude and independence, the freedom to move and dream – aging takes most of it away.

The death wish is the realization that soon it will be you in need of a caregiver. It's the recognition that time is slipping away, and death is essential for you to live again. The death wish is a natural yearning to fulfill dreams before it is too late. In this sense, caregiving is a reminder of the limits of freedom. Freedom doesn't last forever. It's an illusion.

It's not until the last breath - followed by silence - that you give yourself permission to feel, to cry, to reflect, to scream and to live for yourself. After it's over, it's difficult to dream again. Caregiving is a seductive practice that impairs the will to live. It's difficult to live for yourself after caring for another person because their life depends on your presence. It's easy to become seduced into forgetting your right to live, to dream, to rest and love – again. Caregiving attacks freedom by creating new language to justify the loss of freedom.

There's spiritual jargon used to deflect the guilt of the death wish. It's God's will. There is virtue in giving. I'm better for the sacrifice. I'm a better person than before. This is an interpretation of oversimplification. These conclusions annul permission to feel, to hurt and cry. Spiritual language nullifies emotions crying for help and direction by making it holy to sacrifice being human.

The spiritual language of the Church regarding caregiving implies a vocabulary which negates the desire for freedom within the context of sacrifices.

The full understanding of the impact of caregiving involves facing the guilt of the death wish. The influence of the death wish is best unraveled after the last breath. That's when the questions emerge. Questions regarding the meaning of life when your own existence feels like death. Yes, your own death! Recovery from the massive loss caused by caregiving begins with affirming the truth. Something is lost. It feels like death. How do you live when so much has been lost? You can't go back, and there is no way of knowing how to go forward when your own breathing is connected to another person's death.

These are the questions that reveal of absurdity of the death wish. The wish anticipates the restoration of freedom, independence and the fulfillment of dreams. The aftermath of death unearths a new form of death – the continued stagnation triggered by caregiving.

It was misleading to think my daddy would live devoid of misery. It was false to assume he didn't need me to help when aging and sickness made it hard to move. Moving forward requires embracing lessons regarding the days coming soon. These are lessons about false security, the impact of aging and the countless lies involving personal freedom.

Someday, real soon, each of us will need someone to wipe the mess from our bodies and to lift us from the floor when our bodies are too weak to stand alone. Who will stand with us when it's time to go to countless doctor appointments and the steps to the car are too hard to make on your own?

It's difficult to discuss lessons involving death. It's much easier to consider measurables – the work we do, the grades we obtain in school and the things we purchase to make us feel special. The lessons of caregiving force a critique regarding assumptions of success. Aging disturbs notions of achievement. Vitality fades and becomes weakness. Reaching goals becomes making it to the next day without falling. Parenthood is not the same when aging eliminates the will to keep pace. Caregiving exposes the weaknesses of parents and the flaws in their teachings involving adulthood.

Parents teach us to take care of ourselves. Aging teaches a different lesson. What it means to be a son or daughter, a niece or nephew, a grandchild, or a close friend, is challenged by the sickness of a person we know. In most cases, our love for a person clinging to life fuels a passion to be present. There are others who battle the urge to refrain from caregiving due to feelings of rejection and neglect. Why care for this person when they failed to take care of me?

There are lessons in spaces that demand a safe place to share. Caregiving brings to the surface anger, pain, resentment, animosity and a band of other confusing emotions. Caregiving eliminates the walls built to conceal the brewing rage. The indifference crafted by distance, pretending there's too much work and other challenges to find the time to show we care, is no longer a valid excuse. Aging forces a different decision.

Owning the burden of a forced decision is essential for caregivers who involuntary take on the challenge. It's hard saying yes when your heart and personal history offers massive reasons to say no.

Again, caregiving demands a different conversation. To fully understand the joy and pain of caregiving, time is required in pondering the steps taken before accepting the responsibility. Time is needed to deliberate words and actions that stir the will to become a caregiver.

For me, it is the unspoken messages that trigger memories regarding why my daddy is worth my becoming his caregiver. Thoughts of days long before I fully understood what it all means to say yes helps me understand my daddy's love for me, my love for him and what it means to become a better man.

Granting yourself permission to explore lessons involving loss is a vital step toward receiving healing.

8

LESSONS ABOUT SELF-CARE

M y daddy came home after Christmas. I cooked and delivered his Thanksgiving and Christmas meals to satisfy my desire to take care of him. My prayer was for daddy to come home for Thanksgiving and Christmas. My frustration was counterbalanced by daddy's appreciation for the people who took care of him.

"What you gonna do for the people who work here?" daddy asked a few days before Christmas.

The nurses and staff at the Neighborhood at the Tiger were part of what felt like an extended family. Given the time he spent there in his movement between home, hospital and rehabilitation centers, the days spent with them outweighed Daddy's time managing life alone.

I purchased chocolate turtles from the Candy Factory. My daddy was happy with my selection, and the people gobbled them up so fast I decided to purchase more for those who worked the second shift. My daddy's love for the people who took care of him was welcomed by the staff. My daddy was convinced they cared for him like a member of their own family. Like the home health nurses, doctors and friends who took care of my daddy, I sensed a bond that went much deeper than people offering good service because it's what they get paid to do.

My daddy was able to go home on December 30, 2013. A lot had happened since my arrival in October – two hospital visits and four admissions and discharges from two different rehabilitation centers. As much as I hated my daddy's time in the hospital and rehabilitation centers, the drain on my body and emotions would have been far worse if not for the break in caregiving.

I regarded it as God's grace during a time when adjusting to all the changes required space and time to contend with what it all meant. What did it mean to witness the loss of body parts while experiencing guilty for feeling tired and emotionally exhausted? My personal struggles were nothing compared to what my daddy endured before and after my arrival. I fully embraced the distinction between my being tired and my daddy losing the ability to keep moving.

This stage of caregiving exposed the difficulty related to embracing my truth. I found it troubling to own my feelings. I considered it selfish to consider my personal pain. I had no right to complain. My daddy's needs took priority over owning the agony associated with taking care of my daddy. I rejected my feelings and placed them in the category of selfish needs. I had no right to be tired. It's selfish to ponder the desire for intimacy. I regarded it egotistical to wish for the embrace of a woman, space away from my daddy, time away from the vicious cycle of activity and yearning for a break.

Caregiving seduces you into negating human needs. I developed a brutal messiah complex that imagined sacrifices as martyrdom. I deconstructed human desires and visualized sinful pleasures as attacks my calling. I made it evil to contemplate the limits of my humanity by making myself into more than a man. I became my personal saint. My caregiving became the walk of faith tied to a theology that forced the carrying of my cross every day. Every day. I rarely allowed myself to get off the cross.

Sleeping became a nonessential practice. The activities that gave my life meaning became things of the past. My quest to fulfill my foodie interest faded and shifted to preparing food to match my daddy's health needs. My love for music failed to find a way into my daily mediation. My prayer life changed, and my long walks and time spent in parks became an old memory.

Caregiving is the enemy of self-care. Somehow, within less than 200 days, my needs got lost in the quest to put my daddy's needs above my own.

My daddy's time away at hospitals and rehabilitation centers became my time away from the constant toil to reconnect with myself. The tussle to find the old me was complicated by the acknowledgment that the old me died when I decided to come home. Some of what was lost needed to die. Some of it I missed. Most of it became part of an internal grappling involving my need to discover what it means for me to know and understand my purpose.

So much of what it meant for me to claim being human was wrapped in the concept of purpose. The language and activity of the Church forced musing concerning a specific type of calling within the context of God's will to die. I pressed to name and own God's purpose in forcing me to come back home. That's how it felt. God made me do it. I lacked the right to decide on my own.

It felt like God was forcing me to feel pain.

I wonder about the benefit of this type of theological analysis. It is true I was helped by pondering the meaning and significance of love. It helped owning the language of love as a guiding principal during my pity parties. It helped knowing my understanding of my love for my daddy, my love for God and what it means to love myself is heightened through caregiving. It is true that becoming a better person – both for my daddy and myself - is elevated by saying yes to becoming a caregiver. After deciding to become a caregiver, the power of love is all you have left to give.

Caregiving is the activity of love. Sacrifice is a derivative of love. They belong together like grace and mercy, peace and justice and peanut butter and jelly. There is no question that sacrifice is essential in validating the authority of love. Problems arise when the sacrifice tendered by caregivers results in the nullification of self-love. The personal gains cultivated by lessons about loss are surrendered when the lack of self-care becomes a form of suicide.

Daddy came home with an attachment in the area where three toes were amputated. The wound vac was there to help in diminishing the influx and infection caused by his diabetes. The presence of the wound vac added new responsibilities. It made it more difficult for daddy to maneuver through his room. The plastic chord that fastened between his wound and the machine required special attention. My daddy was able to place the wound vac on his walker when he needed to make his way around his room or to the bathroom.

It was vast improvement from the cold night when my daddy kept soiling his sweatpants. Daddy didn't need much help other than assuring the chord didn't detach from the wound vac and stayed out of his way when he walked.

"You watching the game," my daddy yelled from his bedroom.

"Yeah," I answered. "We winning!"

The Missouri Tiger defeated Oklahoma State in the Cotton Bowl by the score of 41-31. The win was secured when Shane Ray returned a fumble 73 yards for a touchdown with 55 seconds left in the game. The Tigers scored 24 points in the fourth quarter. My daddy was excited after he changed the channel back to the game after assuming the Tigers would lose.

The Cotton Bowl win was important to my daddy due to how the Tigers were robbed of a Bowl

Championship Series bid after losing to Auburn 59-42 in the Southeastern Conference Championship game. The bids went to Auburn and Alabama. Florida State won the National Championship with a 34-31 win over Auburn. That game would be played on January 6, and we talked about the possibility of Mizzou winning the National Championship if they had been given a chance to play in the BCS.

"I don't think so," I said after poking my daddy's finger to check his blood glucose level. It was normal, again. There was no need for insulin. He didn't need any all day. It was another good day, a point I celebrated as I went to the kitchen to grab his nighttime medications.

I heard the scream before the thump of his body falling on the floor. I ran as fast as I could. He was laying with his head facing the television with a portable urinal near his left hand.

"I had to pee," he cried. "I tripped on the chord when I grabbed it."

It took time before I could move. I'm not sure how long it took – 30 seconds, a minute, maybe more – but it was too long given the pain I felt when my daddy moaned. The pain was too much for him. It was too much for me to endure given all he did to get back home – again. It didn't take long for me to assume the worse. Something was broken. I knew because daddy couldn't move the leg entangled in the plastic chord connected to that thing used to suck all the infection from his amputated toes.

Something was broken due to something used to help him feel better. How does a person move when the good stuff is used to cause more bad stuff?

I called 911 for help. I was told not to move my daddy. They told me to turn on the outside light and open the door. It didn't take long for them to arrive. Two men and a woman showed up with a bed on wheels. They confirmed my diagnosis. My daddy's femur was broken. The worse penetrated my fears. He's so old. He's. He's. The tall man who seemed to be the supervisor must have heard my fears. He told me it would be alright. Recovery wouldn't be so bad. It happens a lot with people his age. It helped for a few moments.

They lifted my daddy with ease and covered him with blankets. It was cold, and snow painted the roads like one of those post cards delivered to people who love the look of snow. My heart was frozen by something other than the snow.

They placed my daddy in the ambulance. I noticed the lights turned on at our neighbor's houses and the few with doors opened with concerned friends standing at the door. The sound of the siren awakened some from their sleep. My fear came back as soon as they closed the door.

I climbed into my daddy's Ford F-150 to meet the ambulance at the hospital. I turned left unto Banks Avenue near the church where I preached my first sermon. I headed up the hill and turned left on Worley Street as the windshield wipers produced sounds that reminded me of a hip-hop beat. The snow made it hard to see, and my frustration with the snow, the cold and my daddy taking a ride in the back of an ambulance stirred an eruption of tears.

The rhythm of my weeping kept pace with the back and forth motion of the windshield wipers. The wet sensation on my face required the gentle touch of tissues, but both of my hands remained glued to the steering wheel to keep the truck from slithering on the road. No music playing. No one near to share thoughts and fears. Only the sound of the wind, blended with the beat of windshield wipers and weeping, kept me company as I made my way to the Boone County Hospital – again.

The ambulance was backing in when I found a parking space. I parked before remembering my daddy has a handicap sticker. I backed up and parked closer to the emergency room door. I knew my daddy wasn't coming home. I should have parked elsewhere. I should have thought of others who need the space. I should have. I took deep breaths to fight the onslaught of personal attacks. I should have been there to help my daddy get out of bed. I should have known the plastic chord would be a problem.

I cried some more.

I prayed.

I'm not sure if it helped. I pretended it did.

The work of caregiving involves a lot of pretending. Caregivers pretend to be strong when the weakness consumes every move. They pretend to have all the answers when the questions make it hard to think. They pretend to have faith when they're consumed by fears that make it difficult to pray. They smile when they ache. They laugh while crying. They evoke the mood of confidence and courage when they desire a place to hide.

I believed my daddy needed my pretension. I pretended to believe everything would be alright. I needed to believe my daddy was strong enough to overcome this setback, but none of it was true. Caregiving produces pretenders who don't know they're pretending. It's part of going through the motions while lacking the strength to keep moving. You're standing still while pretending you're taking steps forward. It's all an illusion. The part that is real was lost in between saying yes to becoming a caregiver and the second or third visit to the hospital.

Lost were the obvious emotions that come with being broken and discouraged. The fake smile and talk about the presence of Jesus hid the pain baking in my soul. I told myself the pretension was for my daddy. He needed to observe the faith on my face, even if it wasn't real. He needed to recognize my ability to trust in God beyond the circumstances that left me challenged to keep believing all of it is true. The part of me that is a minister wasn't enough to stir the last bit of hope that unraveled the need for me to pretend.

I told myself my pretension was for my daddy, but the truth is I needed to pretend to facilitate a change in the way I handled the situation. I pretended until my joy returned. I spoke in ways that hoped to arouse a will to believe what I said was real. I wanted to believe my daddy could walk again like Ezekiel declared when in the valley filled with dry bones. I read scriptures. I prayed more than twice a day. I wrote sermons to conjure a faith common to what I knew before trouble sucked all my joy away.

I pretended because I wanted to believe God was with us. I wanted to believe God loves my daddy enough to provide some good days in between all the bad news that haunted his ability to move. Why did this keep happening to him? What are the lessons for those who keep going back into the hospital after gaining enough strength to return to a life of just enough pleasure to form a real smile after faking it for too long?

The doctors placed a metal rod in my daddy's leg to replace the broken femur. He returned from the surgery with bandages to help the healing and the same machine to suck the infection from his amputated toes. It was another procedure added to the others to remind me of the myriad of questions lodged in my brain. I wondered if any of it was enough.

They say troubles don't last always. Tell that to a person who keeps faking it while waiting for the words to become true. I kept pretending as I waited for what felt like always to come to an end. I kept smiling and saying the words that matched the phrases of Church folks on Sunday morning.

How long Lord? How long?

Weeping may endure for a night, but my joy didn't come in the morning. Or the next day. Or the next.

I pretended it would be alright. I pretended all was well, in my soul. No matter how hard I preached, prayed and waited for my change to come, all I had to keep me moving was pretending I believed all of it was true.

I kept reading the scripture about only needing faith the size of a mustard seed. I needed more than one seed to help me overcome the challenges of caregiving. I started praying for two when I started wishing my daddy would die. There were moments when I carried guilt because it felt easier if he would die.

9

IN SEARCH OF FREEDOM

The world doesn't stop when a person does the work of caregiving. Things don't slow down to give you time to catch up or take deep breaths because the wind has been sucked from your lungs. The merry-go-round keeps moving and seemingly escalates the pace when you're close enough to take hold of the slippery bars dangling in your face. Once you're ready to grab hold and jump on board, something happens. Something makes it more difficult to keep pace.

Life has a way of catching and forcing you to move before you are ready to jump. I found myself in between wanting to move and begging to stand still. I needed time to heal. It wasn't just the movement of activity related to my daddy's sickness. It was also the emotions stirred by being back home. I needed time to manage the feelings that attacked my spirit in the middle of doing my best to be free. Caregiving has a way of doing that – forcing one to address old thoughts and feeling pushed on a backburner for so long the flame was extinguished long ago. I wonder about the timing of caregiving. It doesn't find you after years of addressing the baggage carried through the years. It happens to press the conversations you don't want to have with yourself.

It's the lesson of caregiving few people talk about. Feeling guilty for not doing enough, while feeling guilty for doing too much. All while failing to find the time to honor the need for space to heal from the madness of doing too much when it doesn't seem to be enough. It's the emotional traumas that feels like a pit too deep to escape. There's the work involved in making sure my daddy was alright. There's the work involved in reminding me of the gifts and work that satisfies my desire to make a difference. All of it is complicated by the work needed to define how I feel when none of the work seemed to be enough.

I took a job teaching journalism writing at the University of Missouri, School of Journalism. It was lousy pay with more work than one human should manage alone. My days became consumed with grading papers, creating writing assignments, quizzes and giving lectures involving the ethics of journalism, how to write ledes, press releases and discussions involving current events. The demands of the job are hard to justify, but it gave me time away from my daddy when being a caregiver was too much to endure.

The work at the J-school added work to the work. Shortly after taking on the responsibility of teaching students, I was asked to temporarily join the ministry team at Bethel Church, a mostly white American Baptist congregation. I saw it as a short-term solution in fulfilling my thirst to teach and preach. My need to engage in ministry was roused by the questions in my head. Where is God? Will things get better and a bunch of other doubts inspired a need for me to preach to myself.

The work with Bethel was another escape from my daddy that fueled guilt. Caregiving does that. It leaves you wondering about the person who needs your care. Caregiving lacks a turnoff button. It follows you when you're not home, at the hospital or rehabilitation center. You think about the care daddy is receiving in your absence. Did he fall? Did he eat lunch? Did he urinate on himself – again. It happens in the middle of a sermon or teachable moment. The thoughts accompany you while walking from the car to the classroom, grading papers or preaching.

My caregiving experience made it difficult for me to live free from the burden of fear. It prompted memories of leaving my children with a babysitter to go on a date with my former wife. Dating became a drill in conquering guilt. My desire for pleasure was met with reminders of my role as my daddy's caregiver. It felt like the cross I was called to bear – alone. Work felt like the abandonment of a superior obligation. Preaching seemed nonessential. My daddy needed me. I needed something more, but it felt like I had no right to embrace my needs.

My entire life and body of work was placed under the gaze of my internalized judgment. All of it seemed to be a mistake – leaving my daddy to obtain a Master of Divinity degree from Duke University, becoming a pastor in Durham, NC, writing columns and all the activism – it seemed pointless given what my daddy needed. I felt the guilt of more than 30 years away in another city. I felt the agony of every fall my daddy took, all the time he cried out in hope that someone was near to pick him up when he was too weak to get up on his own.

I preached on alternating Sunday's at Bethel Church. Bonnie Cassida, pastor at Bethel Church, embraced me and I was officially named co-pastor after six months. The members of the congregation gave little reason for me to believe my being black was an obstacle in their desire to hear me preach. The tension I felt was more related to the mound of cultural differences I found hard to let go. Being at Bethel summoned old wounds of growing up in a city with structures that seemed to limit my dreams.

Being present at Bethel Church was complicated by my desire to be present with my daddy. I failed to consider how all of it was confused by my inability to be present with myself in ways that made it possible to be effective in ministry. Everything was changing faster than I could manage. I needed safe places to scream, to cry, to vent and to allow the bleeding to transform into miracles. Caregiving brews a hidden depression that makes it difficult for a person to understand how they feel. The pain becomes normalized in ways that glamorize picking up that heavy cross.

There's little space to allow the expression of anything that feels distressful. Feeling abnormal becomes the new normal. Not feeling that way summons guilt. All of it is a murky cycle leading in the wrong direction. All lessons are back there – that place long before you decided to come back home. Nothing moves toward the future. The light on the other side of midnight can't be seen. I moved in slow motion with limited understanding of what any of it meant for me.

Clinicians call it depression, but that word fails to fully grasp the sensation of being stuck in a place that denies you the right to feel. I used the word love to frame why I decided to become a caregiver, but can it truly be love when you get lost in the middle of the work? Can it be called love when the will to embrace the future is lost in the continuing activity of self-denial and meaningless activity. What I felt was beyond depression – there was no place for me to feel anything.

It's easy to affirm and embrace love for God and love for my daddy as a primary motivation. Lacking was an ability to fully affirm love for myself reflected in my actions. This is a stage of massive dysfunctional thinking and activity.

This is the stage of caregiving I failed to consider. No one warned me. How could they? It's a different sensation that regulates the inability to embrace new possibilities. I lost my will to love beyond a moment. I refused to grant myself permission to allow a woman to fully enter that space where disillusion and despair needed her to pull me back into a safer place. I needed to be told this is not punishment, and that life, for me, will be restored.

As my daddy healed in a rehabilitation center, on August 9, 2014, Michael Brown was killed by a police officer in Ferguson, Missouri. Brown's death radically shifted the way I approached the work of ministry in Columbia, Missouri. I was compelled to face the meaning and significance of serving as the co-pastor of a mostly white congregation in mid-Missouri. Given the proximity of Ferguson, Missouri to Columbia, Missouri, many of the black students enrolled at the University of Missouri were born and or raised in St. Louis. They were familiar with the place Brown was killed and needed more than "thoughts and prayers" to heal.

Brown's death began a radical shift in how local residents and students talked about race and racism.

The tension brewed like an overheated teapot. The strain on campus was heavy, and it worsened due to the absence of a viable response from the chancellor and system president. Protest on campus mirrored what was happening in the streets of Ferguson. The chat "Black Lives Matter" became a common expression of student displeasure. A series of die-ins halted activity at campus student unions.

Students skipped classes to protest. They forced meetings with the chancellor to discuss their grievances.

While students were fighting to be heard, I continued to preach twice a month at Bethel Church. The tension on campus, coupled with the national attention Brown's death received, complicated my role with the church. I found myself stepping on unfamiliar territory. It wasn't my first time standing before a congregation after the death of a young person. It wasn't the first time I needed to address the questionable actions of the police. It wasn't the first time I needed to address this type of issue as a pastor in Columbia, Missouri.

Brown's shooting reminded me of Kim Linzie, 19, killed by police officers in Columbia, Missouri on July 3, 1985. After arguing with her friend Tammy Mayfield over the use of Mayfield's car, Linzie drove off and Mayfield reported the car stolen. Police recognized the car being driven near downtown, and three police cars chased Linzie before they hemmed the car. Linzie attempted to crush one of the officers between the stolen car and one of the police cars. The police fired 14 shots at Linzie who was killed by a single bullet.

Brown's death felt like de ja vu. This time the protest was generated by students at the University of Missouri. In 1985, I was one of the few students who stood with the family protesting how the police handled the incident. In addition to my role as a journalism student, I served as pastor at Sugar Grove Baptist Church. Serving as the pastor of a black church while completing studies as the first homegrown graduate of the University of Missouri School of Journalism placed me in a unique position. The people I preached to in 1985 knew and understood the need for action to protest Linzie's death. They showed up and marched with members of other black churches. As a journalism student, I felt a brewing conflict between my roles as a journalist and social justice minister.

I found myself entrenched in the middle of conflicting agendas. Before, it was the clash between fighting for justice and impartiality of journalism. It was a critical moment that inspired my decision to focus on ministry versus a serious career in journalism after graduation. This time, it was the conflict between my role as the pastor of a mostly white congregation and my service to black students. Understanding my obligation to the members of the church wasn't enough to inhibit my yearning to support black students while correlating their concerns with those of local residents.

The conversations with the members of Bethel Church were more about the why of protest versus the how to participate. Some were more critical of Brown's role in the shooting. They questioned the actions of protestors. Why did they set fire on buildings in their own neighborhood? Why did they fail to consider the evidence pointing to the officer's innocence? Why, as a Christian, cry "Black Lives Matter" when all lives matter?

The cultural differences are deeper than I assumed. The politics of the membership forced me to think outside of my assumptions as a black liberation theologian. I struggled with finding how to preach and teach in ways that didn't compromise the authenticity of my calling. It felt like God placed me in the middle of an imperfect storm. The nation was watching as Ferguson, Missouri and the University of Missouri defined and, in some cases, redefined the terms and desired outcomes of protest. I grappled with finding my place within this new movement for liberation.

My feelings regarding calling and service was measured within the context of my role as a caregiver. My preaching, teaching, writing and activism was massively limited by my role in assuring my daddy was okay. I lacked the freedom to show up at will. I found myself frustrated by what I couldn't do. When I found time to show up, I left with guilt related to fighting for justice versus being with my daddy. My battle between my former and new roles stirred introspection that made it hard to focus on my freedom.

Freedom.

That's the word that best expresses what happens with caregivers. The tug of war between doing what becomes natural, because it's what has always been done, is met with the doing and sacrifices for the person who demands your full attention. Within the battle between doing what is natural, and sacrificing for another person, there is limited freedom to do what brings comfort beyond all the doing.

The work of the Church and activism represented a different type of caregiving. All of it – caregiving for students, church members and finding a place to fit within the protest movement – strained move- ment toward authentic freedom. The doing thwarts opportunities for freedom. The doing blocks the movement toward being. The emotions generated by the lack of freedom becomes more intense in caregiving. The ways we measure life are altered by a thirst for a freedom that can't be found due to the demands of caregiving and the lack of enough rest.

My caregiving exposed a life dedicated to serving others. I failed in giving myself permission to rest. The doing defined my life in a way that demanded even more than I had given. It was a heavy cross that mandated sacrifices for my daddy and a world worried by needs many are unwilling to give. A lifetime of sacrifice and giving left me drained by the internalized plea to give even more. My decision to become a caregiver deprived me of the freedom to choose rest.

This is an important lesson for caregivers. It's a lesson best understood prior to making the decision to become a caregiver. It's a lesson about counting the cost and avoiding the loss of things that assist in the maintenance of freedom. Freedom is critical in avoiding the weariness that comes when there is nothing left to give due to the demands associated with the doing for others while denying your need for rest. The doing negates the being because of the gift stirred by failing to do enough to offset the regret caused by your absence.

Balance matters.

10

THINGS GAINED

I convinced myself that being a caregiver is about my daddy. I'm not so sure that it wasn't about my own needs. It was about covering the shame related to not showing up sooner. It was about the guilt related to not following the lessons my daddy taught over the years. It was about not becoming the man that made my daddy proud. How could I be that man when so much of what I carried reflected my disdain regarding my actions and inactivity.

Did any of it make a difference? What is the significance of wiping urine from my daddy's legs when there's limited strength left for me? What is the significance of lifting my daddy from the floor other than in convincing myself I'm a good son after spending so many years far away? What is the significance of being present with my daddy when my life is a mess because of my need to face that dude looking at me when I gaze into a mirror?

There's a long list of questions.

Make no mistake, caregiving is about faith. For me, it is about faith in the enduring bond between my daddy and me. It's faith in the love that he shared over the years, and faith that he deserved to be loved in the same way he loved me. My faith in the substance of our father and son union is what compelled me to show up to take care of my daddy. My faith was rooted in a hope that all of it – the loneliness, the weariness – would be resurrected after it was all over. I held a faith grounded in a hope that I would be transformed into a better human being because of my desire to come home.

My faith in my bond with my daddy was not enough. Standing there saturated in cold water forced me to contemplate faith in myself. This is the point where the doing confronts inadequacy. No matter how hard I tried, I didn't have enough to survive. My weakness consumed the moment and my fears controlled my movement. I lacked the patience and fortitude to take another step. My faith in my ability to care for my father vanquished in that chilly moment. In my mind, I couldn't do it.

Could this be the realization that kept my mother away? Is this the consideration that kept my sister from making the two-hour trip to help take care of my daddy? Was it the thought of what they couldn't do, more than their desire to do what they could, that prevented them from becoming my daddy's caregiver? If so, is there validity in being strong and courageous enough to say I can't do it?

Maybe the real heroes are those who say they can't do it. Maybe they understand their limits enough to protect family members from the burden of their imperfections. The chilled water strained my thoughts in a way that made me ponder the absurdity of my decision. Was I doing this to convince myself I'm a good son, or was I doing it because I believed I could make a difference? If I was doing it to make a difference, is there significant reason to suggest my failure in considering my limitations.

The truth is I was too weak to do it. The truth is I had no option but to do it. I lacked the faith in myself. The good news is my faith in God was enough to propel me beyond my limits.

I like to believe my prayer was answered when my daddy snored his way through the remainder of the night. It's what both of us needed. My frailty exposes my complete and utter reliance on God to fix what I can't on my own. I'm not sure what it means beyond creating enough peace for my daddy to sleep through the infection oozing throughout his body. That night gave new meaning to the song that declares "when nothing else could help, love lifted me."

It was a faith beyond my ability to confess faith that carried me through the night. My prayer was more of a cry – the type of utterance that announces I have nothing left to fight back. It was my form of surrender. I was done. I was defeated. I lacked the faith to move beyond the chill of the night; therefore, daddy snoring was the answer to my cry for help. It doesn't take much when there isn't anything else to give.

You can call it a mustard seed moment. My faith was the size of a mustard seed – just enough to make room for a miracle. That's what happened. It was a miracle in the same way my daddy had made it through all those days – alone. In a loving way, God spoke to both of us that night. Our love for one another, mingled with God's love for us, to teach a powerful lesson about overcoming. What is the lesson? When there is nothing left to give, simply lean in, cry a little and embrace the absence of hope. The truth is, God doesn't require our hope. God works best with our tears.

Faith showed up in the absence of hope. That too is a lesson. It's not really faith when the outcome is depended on my own strength. I was seeking hope based on things I could control on my own. Things like lifting my daddy from the bed, changing his clothes and washing the dirty ones after the washing machine decided to spit cold water on my chest. My faith was more about my strength. True faith is discovered when everything falls apart. That's when the absence of hope unveils the true nature of a person's faith. It's so much easier when all of it reflects the things we can control on our own.

That's the spiritual side of caregiving. It demands so much of a person's will to sacrifice that it leaves you pondering the relevancy of the things lost. Is it worth it replaces the assumptions related to why we do it? It's not just because of the love we share. It's also about the guilt and shame carried along the way. Our desire for affirmation, love and respect take center stage to our claim it's the love of God that compels us to sacrifice. We sacrifice from a position of strength. We believe there's enough in reserve to carry us through the things we lose.

I never thought there was more to be lost. I'm thinking of the significance of Jesus' message to his disciples. "If you want to be my disciple, pick up your cross and follow me." That was a call to die. The command was to be placed on the cross, not for a few moments, but until everything within us is lost, even to the point of death. That's the point I missed when I decided to come home. I didn't realize caregiving required my death. All of what I assumed about myself had to die to gain the benefits of being a caregiver. In that sense, caregiving is a deeply spiritual experience.

Some may choose to vacate the spiritual lesson in exchange for lifetime of resentment. Caregiving can instill the type of rage that leaves a person fuming over the thing's others failed to give. Caregiving produces pity parties with participants unwilling to cleanse themselves of the cargo piled on their messy lives. Caregiving is an opportunity to release those heavy bags.

THE FREIGHT I lugged through life required private time with my daddy. My taking care of him was my chance for God to take care of me. Some of my baggage was about things forgotten long ago. Those old thought remained locked deep in my subconscious, forcing the type of decisions that prevented me from embracing authentic freedom. There was so much of my daddy in me – both good and bad – that demanded the type of one on one time essential in taking ownership of the actions preventing me from becoming the man I prayed to be.

The chilly water against my chest was a form of baptism. The moment required more of me than I could give. Moving forward demanded the acknowledgment of how my actions impacted others in my life. That day, my father needed me to be a different type of man. Beyond that day, my children needed daddy to be different than before. Something was missing. I lacked the strength to move on my own, but faith was in the room carrying me – step by step.

Faith had to carry me because I lacked the will and ability to move by faith alone.

It was time to learn lessons about things gained.

11

BROKEN BODY PARTS

It was an infection that caused my daddy to act the way he did that night. He was admitted into the hospital the next day. That nasty red underneath his skin was spreading. Diabetes is an unforgiving illness. Doctors amputated more of his toes. My daddy didn't seem to mind. He took it like a champ. Maybe he knew the day was coming. Maybe he felt the nasty spreading down his leg. Maybe he did a good job of pretending he was okay.

I wasn't.

Body parts aren't meant to be chopped off. I envisioned one hack after another until there was nothing left to take. The toe would be followed by a foot. Then comes the entire leg, followed by – I couldn't take the fear I imagined. I prayed for an infection to eat the infection in his leg. It's an absurd thought, but it's what remained stuck in my head.

When bad things happen, it's always good to find the grace of God. There is something good within all the messiness – right? That good for me was time to breathe. My routine shifted from cooking three meals a day, taking vital signs, injecting insulin, washing clothes and dishes, taking daddy to the bathroom, picking him up from the floor and attempting to sleep to cooking for myself, dressing myself, getting into daddy's truck by myself, finding coffee houses to write in my journal by myself and not being able to sleep at night because I was home with myself.

It's hard determining which is worse – enduring the task related to caregiving or carrying the guilt after leaving my daddy at the hospital to head home. Emptiness traveled through my soul at the conclusion of each visit. The agony of my back and forth ritual of taking care of daddy felt like my service unto God. It felt like the work of the Church. Get up early to pray. Spend time reading the Bible and engaging in meditation. Take time to prepare sermons. Pray for the people and make a list of things to do that day.

It was a new type of spiritual work that settled in my soul like the people who celebrate being martyrs. The pain of it all made it difficult to endure, but it stimulated my need for affirmation. Caregiving has a way of stirring the formation of a new type of identity. The way a person finds meaning becomes attached to the work they do in caring for others. Finding balance is critical. Already, I was making caregiving a form of holy work.

I forced myself to find ways to provide self-care. The local owned coffee houses weren't as good as my favorites in Durham, North Carolina – but I pretended it was enough. I missed the vast diversity that made my life meaningful in Durham. My daddy's home - my old home made home again - was the same as before I left to gain freedom. Like before, I needed an escape from extreme limitations. My time away from my daddy made it more difficult to forget former days.

I missed the woman I still loved. I missed the work and the people. All of it. Caregiving is about missing things. That along with comparing your new life with your former days. Thinking about my daddy made it easier to cope. His experience was much worse than my desire to overcome being homesick.

I keep thinking about lost body parts.

Daddy stayed in mostly in private rooms. Working for an insurance company provided special perks in retirement. Paying for healthcare wasn't a problem. Daddy had more than enough to foot long term stays. The same doesn't apply for those who lack the resources to receive the best care available. My daddy was privileged, but he earned his right to receive the best. He wasn't the stereotypical old black man placing a burden on the system.

My political sensitivities showed up whenever I presented my daddy's medical insurance credentials. Given Missouri is one of the states that refused to receive funding for Medicaid expansion, making it known that my daddy didn't need government support was a source of pride.

It was also a source of internalized tension. My daddy receiving proper care was constantly juxtaposed against my desire to help others receive quality care. This was a point that exposed my own limits. I was one of the others who lacked any form of medical coverage. My daddy's teaching slapped me in the face with every medical visit. My daddy did the hard work of preparing for the future when I failed to do the same to take care of myself.

It wasn't enough to stop the loss of body parts.

My daddy stayed at the Bluffs long enough to expend all the money approved by his insurance for a rehabilitation stay. The pattern involved transferring my daddy to The Neighborhood by Tiger Place, a high rent rehabilitation center on the South side of the city, after time ran out. The Neighborhood by Tiger Place smelled like rich people, unlike other rehabilitation centers that reek sickness as soon as you walk through the door. The updated décor sent a message regarding who had the right to stay. There weren't many black people there.

They placed my daddy in the area where he normally stays. It was on the lower level with staff who knew my daddy by name. They were glad to see him, but wished he wasn't there - again. In their line of work, caring for a person means you hope to never see them again unless it's at church on Sunday morning or the grocery store. Many of the people on staff knew members of our family. That's what happens when you live in a community with a small black population. It seems like everyone knows everyone, or at least someone who knows someone in your family.

Daddy's movement was limited at first. They brought Daddy's food to his room at first. In time, he began receiving physical therapy to help in the adjustment back home. The plan shifted when daddy's hearing worsened. Something was eating inside his ear – another infection. Daddy had to go back to the hospital to amputate more toes.

It reminded me of musical chairs. The only thing missing was music to guide our movement. It began at home. Sit. From there to the hospital. Sit. From there we moved to the Bluffs. Sit. Move to the Neighborhood at the Tiger. Sit. Back to the hospital. Sit. Return to the Bluffs. Sit. Move back to the Neighborhood at the Tiger. Sit. Now, wait to go back home.

In between stays at the hospital and rehabilitation center were a variety of appointments including a wound doctor, Dr. Carolle Silney (his primary care doctor), and a long list of specialists. Daddy had a doctor to monitor his hearing, an internal medicine specialist, a cardiologist and a variety of laboratories to measure illnesses seen and unseen. My daddy's health situation reflected a long history of health-related problems – prostate cancer, meningitis, strokes, heart attacks, diabetes and numerous infections.

I couldn't remember when my daddy wasn't sick. I wondered about the underlying causes. Was it his eating habits? Was it the consequence of too much stress? Living with the death of a daughter could have done it, or maybe it's the outcome of being a black man living in America. Or, maybe it's the byproduct of working numerous jobs for more than 40 years. The life of poor health is the price black men pay for carrying heavy loads on their backs while eating food that causes bad health.

Keeping track of all the appointments is enough to warrant a personal assistant. That along with a chauffeur, personal chef and other staff to keep pace with all the challenges. The demands of care-giving are more than one person can handle on their own. It's takes a village to keep a person healthy. Managing the demands of a sick person can easily result in things falling through the cracks.

My daddy was surrounded by a community of caring people. Candance, a neighbor living in a house that was gutted to fit her needs, spent significant time with daddy before I moved back home. Charles Williams, a childhood friend who still lived in the two-story yellow house across the street, checked on my daddy almost every day. He was the person who found daddy naked on the bathroom floor. Cecil Warren, Jr., my cousin, took my daddy to doctor appointments before I arrived.

I wanted to think all of it was new. The struggles in getting to the bathroom at night, the budding infection on his foot and leg, the nonstop schedule, the ongoing movement between home, hospital, rehabilitation centers and back home – had to be new. It couldn't be the life daddy lived before I moved back home. The truth was painful to face. As bad as it was to maintain all of it, it wasn't new. This is life Daddy was forced to endure before I showed up to fix what was missing. It's what others witnessed. It's what people outside the family helped my daddy overcome.

Considering other people taking care of my daddy challenged me to critique the assumptions of my heroism. I wasn't a superhero. I was not a knight wearing shining perched on a horse to rescue my daddy from evil. Showing up was not enough to offset an extended period of absence.

I wondered if they judged me for neglecting daddy's need for my support. Why wouldn't they question the son of the man who modeled what it means to be a good father? I deserved being weary at night. I deserved the loneliness that came after walking away from the benefits of living in a community with friends and all the perks that come with being free. I was paying the price for living with my freedom. I was free not to care. I was free not to think about obstacles my daddy faced all day and through the night.

I wanted to believe daddy's life reflected things getting worse after I returned home, but it was the same ole same ole he was experiencing long before I decided to come back home.

Living with guilt is unbearable. I'm sure my daddy never held my absence against me. As grateful as daddy was for my being present, I often sensed him wishing I was back in Durham living my life without the drain of taking care of him. As much as my daddy needed my help, it doesn't make it easy to accept the help of your children. The tension between the desire for freedom away from caregiving, and accepting the significance of being present, is where new truths emerge beyond the assumptions we make about caregiving.

The truth finds you after you move past the guilt.

It comes after you embrace the significance of being in that place. To fully embrace the spirituality that comes with caregiving, I had to seek meaning beyond all of it. My being present had meaning beyond taking care of all my daddy's needs. It's not about the tasks I performed or overcoming the guilt I carried for not being present with my parents over the years. There was much more to the lesson than any of those assumptions.

Learning the lesson came upon considering comments people made upon learning I was moving back home to take care of my daddy.

"It is be the hardest thing you'll ever do. It will be the most rewarding experience of your life."

All of that was true, but not for the reasons I expected when I first listened to people share this truth. It was true not because of my doing. It was true because of my being. It's not the labor that makes it the hardest thing and most rewarding thing I've ever done. It's being present that makes it both grueling and gratifying. In this sense, the work of caregiving is a deeply spiritual experience that requires more than a person is capable of envisioning when they first decide to move back home.

The conversations I had with myself began to shift. In the beginning, I questioned why and how I did it. Watching my daddy endure the absence of body parts guided a new form of reflection. I wondered what I would feel if I failed to do it. My being present with my daddy meant far more than the agony of all the doing. I pondered the consuming guilt for those who refuse caregiving. How do they confront their absence of presence after the one they love has died? How do they face their unwillingness to give up personal comfort after numerous calls regarding finding daddy naked on the bathroom floor?

"What would I feel if...?" the thought came to me often after I moved back home.

The second question digs at the quality and nature of my love for my daddy. It breaks through all the language used to convey how we honestly feel. My second question coerced me into considering the validity of my claim about loving my daddy.

"if you really love him, why would you leave it up to others to take care of him?"

Because it's easier, I answered. Because my work is more important, I answered. Because I'm selfish, was the conclusion that dug at my real reasons. It's the truth that would make it challenging to fully forgive myself if I failed to move back home before it's too late.

Being present is essential in affirming the assumptions related to my spiritual practice. Being present isn't just for my daddy. Being present isn't just about offsetting the conversations others may be having about my love for my daddy. Being present is vital in helping me move beyond the language of love toward a practice of love rooted in a willingness to embrace the pain related to the doing. The witness of love doesn't negate the agony of sacrifice. It owns the consequences of doing. More than the pain, love is best expressed through the power of our being. Our being present in another person's discomfort magnifies our awareness and acceptance of love.

In these moments, we know ourselves in ways transcendent of anything we knew before. We become a better version of ourselves. In these moments, we experience what is the most rewarding moments of our lives.

My transformation began when I witnessed my daddy lose body parts. Small parts were taken away in the same way parts of me were taken away. For my daddy, it was parts of his toes. For me, it was a bunch of guilt, loads of fear and the abandonment of my need to control the future. My most rewarding experience is in learning the true meaning of love. After learning this lesson, I will never be the same.

12

LESSONS ABOUT REAL RELIGION

M y daddy's faith was the type you can't keep to yourself. His was not like that of preachers who use religion to make a point about their superiority. They beat the Bible like a tambourine in a way that suggest faith is an old-time religion oozing from fundamentalist theological interpretation. They demanded obedience to their own will, filled with humble submission to their version of truth. There is no place for questioning their brand of religion when the hypocrisy dangling from their reading of the text makes it hard to sing hymns of praise. Some preachers use religion like a weapon. Along the way, they slay distractors by plugging God's judgement against anyone unwilling to affirm their accounting of truth.

My daddy was a life preacher. He allowed his life to speak more than his words. His living sermon felt like a long walk on holy ground. His faith in things beyond what we could see intensified as he aged. He loved the music of James Cleveland, the Gospel recording artist and founder of the Gospel Music Workshop of America. "Peace Be Still" was his favorite among a catalogue of songs that filled his soul like the Holy Ghost.

Daddy stopped attending church services sometime between my transition from middle school to high school. I'm not sure what happened, but the long drive on the church bus to the Mt. Celestial

Baptist Church in McBaine came to an end just as the seeds of the Gospels were planted in my soul. I was searching for something missing. My time singing in the choir, teaching Sunday Church for my peers and listening to Rev. Butler preach, was replaced by the moans of James Cleveland.

Rev. Butler was old when he died. He lived not far from where my cousins and I lived. Once a week, we gathered for the walk across Worley Street to rehearse to sing on Sunday morning. It was fun attending church. Boys in the choir wore marron shirts and gray pants. I can't remember what the girls wore. It was mostly boys in the choir – Doodle Bug, Daron, Gerad, Mert and me – cousin glued by faith and all things boys do in their journey in becoming men.

Daddy stopped going to church after Rev. Butler died. I remember the smell of pigs as we approach the white building on top of the hill not far from the cemetery where my ancestors are laid to rest. I'm told the church was built by members of my family dating back sometime near the end of the Civil War. The members of the church gave up on maintaining the building and moved to the city in hope of gathering more members. The move came after I moved to Durham.

My daddy didn't need church to be a Christian.

God was close to him in the same way the shadow of the Progressive Missionary Baptist Church set on our house at 309 Dean Street. God must have been showing her sense of humor when the church decided to build on the lot next to my family home. My daddy donated enough land for the church to build a parking lot. It was on the space that was once a creek filled in with dirt by the city.

It was the creek that took the life of Ranger, my dog, back in 1973. Ranger got stuck in the bushes one day. He'd been missing. I remember hearing his howl when I woke up one morning. My daddy got him out from the bushes, but there was nothing they could do to save his life. My daddy believed a neighbor poisoned Ranger. He was the best dog ever – a German Shepard that reminded me of Rin Tin Tin. It was my first experience with the pain of death.

That's where they built the church – within footsteps of the house my daddy made into our home and where Ranger died. It felt like Ranger's spirit was there to protect us from all harm and danger. We were close enough to look out the window when the women with big hats walked toward the building. Some carried tambourines and hymnals in preparation for worship. I watched from my bedroom window but stayed away from the place known for setting the sinful captives free.

Maybe my daddy stopped going to church for the same reasons that left me feeling empty. I was mad at God. Death has a way of brewing rage when prayers aren't enough to keep a person from dying. Daddy didn't say much after we got word that Crystal didn't have long to live. She had a tumor the size of an egg on her brain. Crystal, the baby of the family, was four years younger than me. She had a personality that made you think she was an angel sent to nurture your spirit. I was mad at God for taking her life rather than mine. It didn't seem right to take an angel rather than a boy who didn't know what the world would bring.

Death was a mystery. Watching her fade from an effervescent 11-year-old to a comatose 13-year-old aggravated my lingering faith. The mustard seed was lost somewhere between the prayers of those women wearing big hats and her last breath. It happened in the same room where we once watched cartoons and pretended to be Ike and Tina Turner. Her dancing was better than my voice. It didn't matter when two kids, attached by blood and love, found ways to express what words can't say.

I watched Crystal die. The moment of her death felt like mine to share alone. I stepped into my bedroom and cursed God. I took my rage out on everything close enough to launch into the air. It was my personal witness to something meaningful taken away. It was mine to feel. I never considered how my mama and daddy felt. It was there loss as well as mine. I didn't reflect on the pain of a mother who felt the birth of a daughter. I didn't consider the agony of a father upon enduring the loss of his baby girl. I didn't take note of their tears. I didn't listen to their cries. I couldn't. It all belonged to me. It evoked a deep selfishness of what belonged to me – alone.

Since then, I've spent considerable time contemplating what I lost that day. I lost my faith. I lost my willingness to succeed. I lost my ability to trust. I lost my will to live. My truth has been the subject of sermons, columns, books and poems, but I never stopped to consider what my sister's death meant to my parents. It changed them too.

Maybe it changed them more than it changed me. Maybe. How can you know when your life is tainted by the pain you carry -alone?

Maybe it's why my daddy stopped going to church. Maybe it's why my mama depended on the church for her strength. It could be that my father's pain kept him from trusting God with his attendance. It could be that my mama needed to attend church to remind her of God's enduring presence. For my daddy, it could have been too painful to show up. For my mother, it could have been too chilling not to show up. For me, it was too painful to consider a loving God after the death of Crystal. It didn't help that Ranger died over there.

My steps back to God, after my sister's death, feels like a miracle. I didn't find God – God was always there for me. Always. Through every mistake. Within every attempt to hide pain with drugs and sex. Within every thought of giving up on life because of my unwillingness to face the root of the pain. That is a miracle. It's the miracle of God's love and the significance of God's grace. My journey from confusion to ministry is a miracle. This I know to be true.

But, what about my daddy?

Our Sunday family ritual was to gather at my parent's house after church. Daddy stayed home to prepare the feast. The spread consisted of two meats and multiple side dishes. Daddy cooked with the sound of Gospel music setting the ambiance for space set for a family to celebrate one another. Something was different on that day.

Kathy, my wife, and King and Lenise, my children, noticed the difference when we walked through the door. There was the absence of the smell of food cooking. No James Cleveland hushing the choir in the middle of "Peace Be Still". I inhaled deep to sense the smell of roast beef and baked chicken. Nothing. The kitchen was dark. No sound of pans clinging. Daddy wasn't there.

My mama went to another church that day. Her normal seat at Progressive Missionary Baptist Church was occupied by someone else. Her car wasn't parked in the driveway sending the message it would take time for Mama to drive back home versus walking the few steps to the parking lot joined to my daddy's property.

Both Mama and Daddy weren't home.

Mama pulled up after we walked through the house to confirm daddy's absence.

"Daddy," all of us said with great anxiety.

I walked around the house. No Daddy. He wasn't in his garden in the backyard. He wasn't grilling or smoking meat on the patio.

"Where's your daddy," Mama asked shortly after entering the house. It didn't take much for her to notice his absence.

"We don't know. I thought he might be with you," I answered.

We deliberated on Daddy's absence. Maybe he went fishing. Maybe he…

Daddy walked in the house in the middle of our joint pondering. Something was different. He was wearing a suit. He was dressed like it was time for church on Sunday morning. It made sense. It is Sunday and a church is only a few steps away. More than his suit and tie, something else was different. It was the way he walked. His face glowed in a way that reminded me of what the Bible says involving those in the presence of holiness. The room felt like holy ground. Something was different about daddy. I knew it was something good because it felt like everything stopped to declare Daddy's home.

My Daddy was crying.

He approached me in a way that declared something had changed. For the first time, at least the first time I could remember, my Daddy hugged me. Tight. Tight like he knew I would understand. He hugged me like a person confronted with the change that comes in making a meaningful decision.

"I accepted Jesus today," he said.

I was shocked by my daddy's statement. I always assumed my daddy knew the Lord. I never considered his need to accept what had, in my mind, been accepted. I assumed he had a deep bond with God. I assumed it was that bond that carried him through those many trails, troubles and snares we sing about on Sunday mornings. I assumed his love affair with Gospel music to be an affirmation of a faith deeper than his lack of attendance at church. I assumed that our weekly agape feast was his service to God and family.

His tears told a different story.

This was the day my daddy released the pain. In that moment, I felt my daddy's spirit pour into mine. The hug served both of us in ways that bonded our journeys in informing a new collective identity. Father and son were renewed together in a way that prepared both of us for

what would come later – much later. We didn't know it then, at least I
didn't, but in a deeply mystical way, a lesson was being taught
regarding how our faith involved more than our individual grappling
to recognize the presence of God.

Holding my daddy felt good.

I wept with my daddy because I understood what it meant to allow
God to expose the transforming power of joy - joy that takes you back,
way back, while standing in a moment that reveals the undeniable
presence of renewing energy. I felt the sadness of a father after
enduring the death of his daughter. I felt my coping to overcome the
madness caused by my mistakes. I felt covering pain with substances
while running from the love of God. I felt the joy of renewal that can't
be explained by anything other than knowing God never leaves or
forsake those she loves.

"I accepted Jesus today," was enough to send me down a path of
memories about how I felt when I said yes to letting go. If felt like we
held each other longer than we did. I felt the emotions of my mama as
she shouted with joy. My children, both under the age of seven, knew
something good was happening, but they were too young to understand. My wife moaned with an approval that fought back the urge
to shout.

We call of that the power of the Holy Ghost. Those are the terms
used to explains things too mysterious to understand. Everything
changed on that day. We never talked about it. There was no need to
share the meaning of an experience that is deeper than words. The
embrace and tears were enough. This was time set aside for father and
son to linger together in a way that set both of us free to experience
something greater. The glue was the faith we shared and a love greater
than the scars formed on our broken hearts. Somehow, we knew the
bond between father and son would carry us beyond all forms of
misery. It was the beginning of our change, and that change set us both
free to prepare for a new journey.

I often wonder if my faith helped lead my daddy to Jesus. I'm
certain that my daddy's unspoken faith helped me find my way. That
day changed the way I think about my life and witness of faith. To this
day, I'm troubled that my daddy never witnessed me preach a sermon.

Sure, he listened to recordings of my sermons and read some of my columns, but my thirst was for him to hear me preach.

I'm not sure why it mattered so much. During my daddy's last days on earth, I thought about the trip I made with members of the Orange Grove Missionary Baptist Church to Missouri. We rented a bus and travelled more than 900 miles because of my desire for my daddy to hear me preach. When we arrived, I discovered Daddy was too ill to attend. It felt like a wasted trip.

My disappointment followed me until the end. I wanted Daddy to witness my change. I wanted him to experience the work of God in me. I now know that Daddy stopped going to church because of his inability to sit through worship services. His ailing body was too weak to stay. His desire to attend never faded. His mind was willing, but his body was too weak.

It's one of the complications that comes with aging and illness. Although my daddy lived close to the church, his relationship with the community of believers was obstructed by his lack of attendance. It's a lesson I was forced to learn the hard way. As a pastor, it's easy to become overburdened and focused on the people who show up on Sunday morning while forgetting the sheep who can't make it to church because their bodies are too weak to make the trip. Witnessing the lack of concern coming from the leadership of my daddy's congregation baffled me. The visits could be counted on one hand. There were limited phone calls.

The pain of my daddy's frustration could be felt. He consistently made excuses for the lack of attention coming from members of his church. The failures of my daddy's pastor exposed my shortcomings. The list of senior citizens, and others homebound due to illness, that I failed to consistently visit, haunts me. The immense burdens of managing the work of a large congregation made it easy to place them on the backburner.

When my daddy died, I discovered something worse than the apathy of church leadership in visiting my daddy. I discovered his confession of faith was not enough to sustain his church membership. In the mind of the chairman of the deacon board and the pastor of the church, my daddy's membership was attached to his attendance and giving. Daddy's membership was invalidated when he failed to show up on Sunday and when he stopped paying his tithes and offerings.

This reality came to bare when I called church leaders after my daddy's death. It was the families desire for the funeral service to held at the church where he accepted Jesus. As I made the agonizing call to the chairman of the deacon board, I reflected on the day daddy hugged me while crying because he came to Jesus during the worship service. I envisioned a funeral surrounded by church members. I contemplated the powerful witness of the choir singing "Peace Be Still". Already, I had pondered the eulogy I would preach. Given it's the church where I began my own ministry and where I was ordained, the funeral would be a celebration of how my daddy's life and faith impacted my work in ministry.

As the phone rang, I thought of the land my daddy donated to the church to expand their parking lot. I was flooded with memories of playing on the ground made holy when the church was dedicated in 1976. I thought about Crystal's faith before she died, and my mother and Crystal being charter members of the church.

The deacon answered the phone.

After sending his thoughts and prayers, the deacon shared the policy of the church.

"Your father hasn't been to church in over a year, and he hasn't paid his tithes," the deacon said. "So, it will cost you $500 to use the church for the funeral."

My response reflected my rage. $500 after all my daddy had done for the church. $500 after my mother became a charter member. $500 after my being in the group of ministers to become the first ordained by the church. $500 because my daddy couldn't make it to church. $500 because I failed to pay his tithes. $500 after no visits from church leadership after all my daddy gave to the church.

My rage was accompanied by tears. Why? Because it was a challenge to the claim of my daddy's witness of faith. It minimized the integrity of that moment my daddy hugged me with tears because he accepted Jesus that day. My rage and tears divulged the ache of a son who stood with his daddy as a caregiver. I considered daddy's desire to attend church. I listened as he answered his own questions regarding why no one from the church came to visit. I felt his need for spiritual guidance and support from his church family.

Why should we pay $500 to cover the church's neglect?

There's a lesson for me and other pastors. My contempt toward the church was a critical reminder of the role and responsibilities of the local church. In retrospect, the policy of the Progressive Missionary Baptist Church is not distinctive. Other congregations have procedures regarding the management of facilities for funerals. Others define membership based on attendance and giving and make judgments on how much to charge to bury a loved one.

This is a lesson related to how these policies impact how a family feels after parents die. There are other lessons about how daddy's faith changed the way I think as a man. Maybe it would help Church Folks to think more about how death impacts the faith of caregivers.

The first lesson involves my daddy's tears. I didn't see my daddy cry when Crystal died. I'm sure he cried, but I was too engrossed in my own pain to notice. Tears are tears, but there is a vast difference between a man crying because of pain and when joy stirs those tears.

Hugging my daddy while he cried has made it easier for me to cry. Boys are often taught crying is a sign of weakness. There is strength in a man crying for all reasons, but there is something incredibly special when a man shows emotions based on his relationship with God. When that happens, crying is about the love. The tears reflect memories regarding God carrying us when we lack the strength to move. Seeing my daddy cry encouraged me beyond what I preach. The older folks used to call it "the fire shut up in your bones". Paul Tillich called it "the acceptance of being accepted".

My daddy's tears prepared me for what would come later. This memory rekindled my spirit when I found myself wounded by my decision to become my daddy's caregiver. As much as I love my daddy, the weight of caregiving has a way of forcing questions. Why did I do it? How did I survive it? Why me and not someone else? Where are other members of the family to support me? Why me Lord, take this cup from me. The memory of my daddy's tears provided the answer to these and other questions. The tears spoke to a will beyond my own. I was called to serve my daddy in the same way I was called to serve the Church.

My daddy hugged me that day. He sought me out because of the need to make a statement to his son. It was my moment of change, like a rite of passage, that hug spoke to my role as my daddy's spiritual partner. I like to think my walk of faith helped my daddy make his decision. That hope helps me embrace being daddy's caregiver. It means more when placed within the context of holy duty. Caregiving helps us understand what it means to be set apart to embrace a radical call on our lives.

When Jesus told us to pick up a cross and follow him, it implies a radical commission to die. We are not called to take a vacation on the cross. It is the place in which we die for others. We go because we concede the promise of the resurrection, but death is painful. There is no comfortable way to die. It hurts. The moments before the last breath are the hardest part. In time, death becomes a better option compared to dealing with the agony of declining heath.

Hugging my daddy bonded us in a way that established the terms of my future. My daddy's tears became my tears. My daddy's relationship with God transformed my relationship with God and my father.

From that moment moving forward, my obligation as a Christian, and my daddy's son, drove in my spirit my need to carry my daddy's cross. My daddy's witness became my witness. My daddy's life became a reflection of my life. My daddy's sickness became my own. My daddy's will to cling to life, long enough to gain the courage to die, was the cross we carried together.

We are tricked into thinking life is what we do in stages. We enter the world depended on others for survival. In time, we learn to live on our own before relying on others to take care of us – again. The space between dependence and independence is viewed as the better years.

Caregiving taught me the fallacy of our assumptions. The best years are when we need others to carry us because we are too weak to walk alone. The truth in this witness is found in the lessons that nurture us along the way. All of it matters. All of it matters in making us partners in the quest for understanding.

My journey of faith is tied to my father's pursuit for understanding.

Somewhere long before I was born, my daddy learned a lesson about freedom. He discovered freedom on a hill in a church called Mt. Celestial Baptist Church. My daddy learned the lesson through the life of his own daddy. The struggles of life complicated his passion to affirm the lessons of freedom. Caregiving rekindled lessons involving freedom setting us free to embrace love.

Faith in God is what we do together. When I was born, my daddy promised to stand with me. When my daddy died, I placed my cross beside my daddy's and released his spirit to God.

13

THE LOVE FEAST

Things were going great for my daddy after he returned from the rehabilitation center with a rod in his leg. It took him four months to walk comfortably. I claimed it to be a miracle.

I celebrated by daddy's return home with a birthday party. On November 7, 2014, I hosted a feast for my daddy. It was part birthday party, he turned 78, Thanksgiving and a community agape feast. It was my version of what my daddy did before he was too sick to continue the tradition. I cooked a turkey, collard greens, dressing, candied yams, macaroni and cheese, sweet potato and apple pies, yeast rolls and fried catfish.

I invited everyone I knew connected to my daddy and mama. Reverend Roderick Williams, pastor of Progressive Missionary Baptist Church, showed up along with other members of the church. I bit my tongue while thinking about them coming to eat while failing to show up to check on my daddy. It felt like payback for all the times I failed to visit senior citizens before they died. I couldn't point to the speck of sawdust in their eyes when I had a plank in my own. Some lessons are best learned when the shoe is placed on your own feet.

Most of the people came to see my mama. I gladly made the two-hour drive to Waynesville, Missouri to bring her home. My daddy's love for my mama was not diminished by their separation. They remained married, and my daddy continued to pay her bills.

"When I said I do before the Lord, I meant that," he kept saying it. "Nothing will change the way I feel about your mama."

Church members and friends came to welcome her back home. It didn't seem to bother my daddy that a handful of people came to check on him. Daddy was happy his wife was home in her element among friends. It felt like old times, but something was missing.

Sandra, my sister, drove from Kansas City with a friend. Missing were my three children, my nephew, niece and their children. It was enough to make my daddy happy after so much time spent between the hospital and rehabilitation centers. It's what he did before the sicknesses robbed him of the ability to stand in front of a stove all day. It felt like I was handed the torch from my daddy. It was another reminder of how so much of my daddy is locked up inside of me.

The wife of my mother's new pastor showed up to say hello. It was one of those moments that felt like folks checking in to assure their church member wasn't staying. She made the long drive from Waynesville but refused to eat my food. She gave me that look that suggested something is wrong with my cooking. She perched her noise high in the air denoting an assumption of being better than the other people in the room. I was tempted to make a statement laying out all my credentials, but respected my mama's desire to respect her pastor's wife.

There were numerous lessons lingering around the house. I thought long and hard about the merit of teaching a class at divinity schools aimed at preparing people for conducting home visits. Instruction involving the importance of talking to my daddy before eating my food, showing respect to the person who cooked the food and making assumptions about my food would help people who lack appropriate home training. I wanted to scream the day was about my daddy returning home after a long stay in the hospital and rehabilitation center, versus my mama's return home for a brief visit. It's the type of real-world teaching that diminishes the likelihood of a person losing their religion in the middle of thinking, "no she didn't" followed by an assortment of four-letter words.

Daddy spent most of the time in his bedroom versus taking his favorite seat in the living room in front of the electric fireplace I purchased for him while he was recovering. I selected one like the fireplace in the dining room at the rehabilitation center. He told me he wanted one, and I found it at the Lowes not far from the rehabilitation center. I replaced his favorite damaged chair with a new Lazy Boy. It was equipped with in seat lift control that made it easier to get out of the chair.

My goal was to make my daddy's return home more comfortable than when he left. I did my best, with the help of Deborah, to plant flowers in the front. Before getting sick, my daddy was known for his gardening skills. A professional photographer stopped by one day to record my daddy's skills with pictures fit for a lawn and gardening magazine. The back yard looked like a botanical garden. The front yard resembled a rose garden. I did my best to replicate what we saw in those pictures, but I lacked my daddy's patience and green thumb.

None of it – the fireplace, the new chair, the flowers in the front yard, the food, the people – was enough to get my daddy to leave the safety of his bedroom. Rather than being a reminder of how things used to be before the sickness stole years from my daddy's life, the day recapped lessons regarding how things would never be the same.

My daddy didn't cook the food. The flowers weren't planted by daddy. He wasn't in the middle of each conversation telling jokes and stories that left every grasping for air due to their laughter. It didn't feel like my daddy's home. His presence was limited to his bedroom. There was an emptiness that exhibited the loss of a meaningful marriage. The clock continued to tick on the time spent together – more than 55 years – but the magnitude of my Mama and Daddy's union didn't feel the same.

The party was not a celebration of vows taken long ago, and the conjuring of memories that proved the merit of two lives joined with the promise of until death do us part. The party wasn't about supporting my mama in her quest to take care of my daddy and being thankful for Daddy being back home to find peace in the place they call home. The eating of food was not a salute looking back and forward at the intensity of a love capable of overcoming the burden of sick days. The party was not a recognition of my mama and daddy's love. It was an observance of my mama's return home to witness my daddy coming back to the place she left in the middle of my daddy's struggle to heal.

Staying in his room symbolized an expanding gap. The love remained, but the distance between my mama and daddy shattered the intended focus of the day. It was supposed to be about coming home. It wasn't. It's hard to come back home when the home you worked hard to create is not the same because of who walked away.

It wasn't my mama's fault. Her love for my daddy remained beyond the distance created by her departure. My mama didn't leave because of my daddy. She left to claim her right to live. My mama's inability to continue as my daddy's caregiver isn't a reflection of tarnished love. It's more of a manifestation of the pain stored by an aging couple grappling to determine ways to survive when everything they know changes.

Months later, I learned a profound lesson regarding the meaning of home. My daddy grappled with finding his way back home. Home, for my daddy, was the place he worked hard to create for his wife and children. It reflected his understanding of his roles as a father, husband and man. My daddy embraced what he understood as his responsibility as provider and protector. My daddy understood home as the place where he paid all the bills on time, worked hard to keep a roof over our heads and clothes on our backs. The rifles and pistols, locked in the gun case in the family room, were there as a reminder of my daddy's willingness to kill anyone who harmed my mama, my sisters and me.

Home was about my daddy's strength. It was conveyed when fish, rabbit, squirrel, deer and other animals were killed, skinned and cooked. Home was about my daddy working harder than he should to do all he could to make our lives comfortable. Home was my daddy's love.

It didn't feel like home anymore.

"All I ever wanted to do was make sure you and your mama had everything you need," is the statement that remains glued in my memory. "I didn't want anything for myself, other than a truck and a place to fish."

My daddy's version of home was tarnished long before my mama left to begin a new life in Waynesville, Missouri. Home for my daddy was intertwined in his conception of manhood. Home is not the same when the power to provide and protect is exchanged for the help of a caregiver. The people in my daddy's house may have conjured memories of how life felt before home was stolen by sickness.

It was the last time my daddy's house would be filled with people before he died. The pastor and friends from the church didn't come back. My mama and sister returned to their own homes. I removed the food from the tables and washed the dishes. There was no dishwasher, so all of it was done by hand. I made to go plates for the people who enjoyed my cooking. Afterwards, I placed the leftovers in the refrigerator. I worried about keeping daddy away from food that would raise his blood sugar levels. I made plans to give him what he could eat and to eat the rest myself.

I scrubbed the countertops with Lysol antibacterial kitchen cleaner spray. I used the same cleaning product for the stove top. I wiped both tables – the one in the kitchen and the one in the family room – with Murphy's oil. Cleaning provided the release I needed after all the cooking and entertaining. It felt like I seized my daddy's old role of cooking and cleaning during family gatherings.

Then it hit me.

My daddy was more than a provider and protector. My daddy is my role model regarding what it means to be a man. More than that, accepting the role as my daddy's caregiver helped me understand how to be a man inspired by my daddy's lessons.

Caregiving changed my view of God. My awareness of the work and power of God is no longer lodged in my conception of the work I do but is now understood through the power of my "being". It's not what I do, but it is who I am that makes a difference.

The blessing of caregiving is in being present with people you love. This understanding frees me to find strength in what is lost versus clinging to what I can't control.

Caregiving granted me permission to accept how my faith is linked to my father's faith. Like my daddy, the way I express my faith is through serving others. My understanding of my purpose is influenced by lessons learned in watching my father serve others. My service to others, like my daddy, is how I show love. Caregiving for my daddy was deeply rooted in my will to return what I have received.

My relationship with the Church, and feeling rejected by members of the church, is expressed best as a continuation of what I have sensed with my daddy. In these ways, my connection with my daddy is reflected beyond physical measures. Caregiving for my daddy unveiled deep spiritual bonds which surpass the burden of things lost. The common bonds revealed in caregiving prove the point of the people who share their experiences regarding caregiving.

It is the most impactful decision a person can make.

I am my father's son.

It's the lesson of a promise fulfilled.

14

LESSONS ABOUT ASSUMPTIONS

I 've always loved my daddy, but I didn't always know why. That's not a bad thing. Love is hard to define. You think you know love and then it changes. You discover the love you thought you knew is nothing in comparison to the love that finds you in vulnerable places. My love for my daddy was always in conflict with massive contradictions. My struggle to define what it meant for me to be a man was held in the delicate balance between the parts I rejected and the parts I wished to model as a man.

My daddy was willing to assimilate into white culture. I was more informed by Malcolm X than Dr. Martin Luther King, Jr. My daddy was content with hope in the American Dream. I anticipated the coming of a revolution that redefined life in America. My daddy feared my activism. I feared the continuation of massive hypocrisy and disparity. My daddy lived with his spirit glued to reminders of black limitations. I was groomed in messages of black pride and unlimited possibilities.

My pre-college years with my daddy were whittled by vast differences stirred by changes in the black community. Those changes were exposed for all Americans to see. It was the age of being sick and tired. Black Americans were split ideologically and tactically. Some embraced the philosophy of nonviolent resistance. Some adopted

Malcolm X's desire to improve life among black people "by any means necessary". My daddy took another position. He avoided the issue. He rejected the cry for Black Power and liberation. My daddy stood on the sideline while his son jumped in the middle of the fray with a determination to set all black people free.

The 1970's redefined life in black America. The declaration of self-determination was met with defiance among those challenged by memories involving the consequences of fighting back. My daddy was groomed during the decades of white domination. He knew stories of black people dangling from trees like strange fruit. My daddy's learned lessons about avoiding the fury of white people bent on keeping black people on the bottom. I wasn't afraid. I stood with Muhammad Ali's refusal to honor being drafted to fight in the Vietnam Conflict. My daddy stood with Joe Frazier against Ali when they fought on March 8, 1971. Still in elementary school, I knew enough to embrace Ali's willingness to stand against white supremacy.

My daddy's desire for my life was in direct conflict with my own. Our differences emerged when I raised questions regarding my reading of the "Little Black Sambo" books written by Helen Bannerman. My daddy questioned my disdain when I asked question about why Tarzan, a white man, was the "King of the Jungle". I found it hard to accept the absence of people who looked like me on the most popular television shows – "The Beverly Hillbillies", "Leave it to Beaver", "Green Acres" - and most of my Saturday morning cartoons. My daddy's reluctance to address my queries made it hard to embrace him as my role model.

Black life in America is complicated. My daddy's unwillingness, or deep-seeded fear, in addressing the concerns, was offset by his undeniable strength. These are lessons involving survival in the face of extreme opposition. My daddy taught lessons passed down from generations of black people forced to bow when tempted to stand. My daddy taught lessons about trust, commitment, hard work, perseverance and fighting the desire to fight when doing so has consequences that impact your children. These are lessons involving the other side of protest. What profit is there for the man who fights a white man only to die with children in need of their daddy to pay the bills?

Caregiving forces a deep gaze back into the lessons you couldn't hear when your perception was tainted by divergent ideologies. Looking back exposes a long list of failures that resulted in being overly glued to reasons that make it difficult to listen. I thought I knew more than my daddy. His ways were too old-fashioned to honor. His view of life for me was an outdated mandate that required embracing the "white man's" understanding of roles black people should assume as part of their place within the American Dream.

I called my daddy's dream a nightmare. I refused to listen. I was afraid of shouldering the life of my daddy's limitations. I desired more for myself and my children. I was ashamed of his vocation and feared becoming a janitor. I was unable to listen to my daddy's faith in my achieving great things. I witnessed his brokenness and feared doing the same – work, work, work with no rest to explore life beyond paying the bills. My daddy kept teaching. I was unable to listen.

Caregiving changes everything. It forced me to listen to the lessons beyond the assumptions I made regarding my daddy's limitations. Caregiving exposed my daddy's strength. My shame in what I perceived as my daddy's "Uncle Tom" ways transitioned into a pride in my daddy's ability to survive. Like Joe Frazier's boxing style, my daddy bobbed and weaved through life. He placed relentless pressure on his opposition. When forced against the ropes, my daddy used a powerful left hook. My daddy didn't talk much. While in the ring called life, he punched his way out of danger until knocking out his adversary.

My daddy loved boxing. His love for Joe Frazier epitomized his personal battle regarding how people measured black identity. Ali turned the fight against Frazier into a cultural and political referendum. Ali was the champion of the black revolution and Frazier was the white champion cloaked in black skin. Frazier felt isolated from the black community. In today's terms, Frazier wasn't "woke" enough to be named the champion of black people.

My admiration and support for Ali must have struck a nerve with my daddy. The attack he felt was comparative to what Frazier carried in the ring against Ali. Frazier was the champion of the black people who wanted to be left alone to do their job. Frazier fought on behalf of the black men standing on the sideline in the battle for justice and equality. My daddy cheered for Frazier to teach me a lesson about black identity. He was no less a black man because of his allegiance. He was a black man seeking affirmation in his pursuit to teach me lessons involving how to stand when faced with numerous enemies.

My daddy supported Frazier because he was a black man. He supported Frazier because he was attacked by a black man. Frazier was criticized for not taking a political position. My daddy was under attack by me and other youth who lifted Ali as their champion. We embraced the message of Ali. We dismissed men like my daddy.

Caregiving helped me understand the pain of my daddy's decision. My life and work unearthed the brutal pain carried by men like my daddy. The 1970's began an era that radically shifted the terms that define black manhood in America. My daddy was nurtured within a culture that lifted notion of black manhood as the provider and protector of his family. Strength was defined by hard work and a willingness to endure whatever it takes to shield the family from the vicious attacks against the black family.

The transition involved images of black men as athletes, entertainers, pimps and activist. These images evolved through black exploitation movies, sporting events and the advance of the black-owned music and media industry. The strength of black men was reflected in images of defiance. It was expressed by black men fighting to redefine masculinity through the black nationalism movement. The Black Panthers, the Southern Nonviolent Coordinating Committee (SNCC), the Nation of Islam, and other groups, provided America a new view of black manhood. Black men were rioting across America to make a clear statement regarding enough being enough.

Blaxploitation films, like Sam Greenlee's "The Spook Who Sat at the Door", were influenced by the Black Power movement. 'Sweet Sweetback's Baadasssss Song" incorporated Black Power ideology by allowing actors to be the stars of their own narratives versus assuming subordinate roles. "Shaft" incorporated black political and social issues in the plot. John Shaft exposed black culture to mainstream America while incorporating black power and Marxist themes. These films were set in poor urban neighborhoods and utilized violence, sex and the drug trade to provide viewers a glimpse of black communities struggles in overcoming "The Man". Words like "cracker" and "honky" were used to express the angst black people felt in being oppressed by white people.

These films redefined what it means to be a black man in America. My daddy taught lessons about survival. These films stirred my generation to embrace a different type of masculinity. We wanted to protest like Dr. King. We wanted to resist like Malcolm X. We wanted to create a new economy to build wealth and security. In many ways, these new images of black manhood distracted from the emphasis on marriage and parenthood, leaving the life and teaching of my daddy a subtext to the model of black manhood in America.

Caregiving forced a critical gaze related to my understanding of what it means to be a black man. The teachings of my father failed to generate the expected outcome of a man dedicated to teaching lessons that impact the life and survival of the black family. My caregiving exposed the massive gap between my daddy's teachings and my inculturation into an evolving understanding of black masculinity. Taking care of my father forced me to ponder all that has happened to the black family in America. As much as the demise of the black family is about the manipulation of redlining, the re-segregation of public education and institutionalized racism lifted in Richard Rothstein book The Color of Law: A forgotten History of How Our Government Segregated America, how we witness and own the transference of black manhood from generation to generation is influenced by the vitality of black life and the family more than we have assumed.

Caregiving minimizes the massive divide caused by assumptions fashioned by generational differences. What I perceived as the limits of my elders is the language of our deliverance. Their weakness is our strength when set against our joined effort to confront the damage caused by the limitations enforced by white privilege and institutionalized racism. Caregiving challenged me to end the labeling and critique of my father's version of manhood to grasp how our varied ideological positions were used to build an enormous wall between a father and son. My generation's reconsideration of the merits of black manhood complicated our will to listen.

My daddy's acceptance of Frazier was met with my dismissal of my daddy's version of authentic black masculinity. Caregiving helped me comprehend how my daddy's support of Frazier was a plea to be seen in a growing movement to dismiss his interpretation of black male identity. My support of Ali was viewed as a rejection of his masculinity. Caregiving for my daddy was a rapid movement toward death and the enduring cry to be heard before the coming of my daddy's last breath. The lesson was to embrace the messages lost long ago in our maddening quest not to listen. Our desire to be right became more important than the undeniable witness and authority of what it means to be family.

My daddy's lessons involving how to be a husband and father were diminished in my mission to reinvent what it means to be a black man living in America. I sought manhood through power, a radical revolution and through activism. My daddy was determined to teach me how to be a man by serving a family.

Caregiving forced me to listen.

I think my daddy knew I needed his lessons. In many ways, I think my daddy knew I needed more to prepare me for his death. The Bible talks about lessons passed down from our ancestors. It's why they pour libations in African religions. We miss out when we move with the wisdom in our imaginations. My daddy must have known I needed more than the lessons in those books I read about black people in search of a revolution.

My desire to listen to my daddy's lessons began in 2001. I was on a sabbatical leave from the Orange Grove Missionary Baptist Church. It was during that sad season following the completion of Preacha' Man, my first novel. I was coping with what to do with the book. It was far too risky to be sold in a traditional Christian bookstore, but I felt the need to publish it due to the issues within the book. It was my story and I knew publishing it could lead to the end of my work within a traditional Baptist congregation. I needed my daddy's wisdom for what felt like the first time in a long time.

Maybe my daddy knew I needed his wisdom.

Glenda, my girlfriend at the time, and I pulled up at the drive-in window at a McDonalds to purchase Frappuccino's. We joked the caffeinated drinks were like crack cocaine for both of us, and, after the long journey, we needed a hit before making our way to my daddy's house.

My daddy had recently been released from the hospital after a

series of strokes. It was the time after he decided to retire from Shelter
Insurance Company. He left his job of mopping floors at his second job
at the elementary school after getting a promotion into management.
Gone were the long days of working two jobs to pay the bills. Playing
by the rules was rewarded with work that granted him the power to
hire and fire people. The strokes ruined the blessing of work that must
have felt like life on the other side of the river.

My daddy answered the door with a smile that suggested he was
glad to see us. He was waiting for us, and dinner was ready. Mama
was there to welcome us home. The Frappuccino's helped us linger
long enough not to give the impression we were too tired to embrace
my daddy's midwestern hospitality.

Daddy was up early the next morning and moved like a man on a
mission. I could feel a lesson coming to help me through my crisis. My
daddy told us he wanted to take us out to eat. That wasn't the lesson,
but there was something about the way he moved that gave me reason
to believe something good was coming my way. The uneasiness caused
by the long drive and concerns regarding my daddy's health, faded as
I watched him move like a man determined to teach me that lesson.
Mama said he hadn't been out of the house. The stroke had taken his
determination to step outside long enough to feel the breeze and the
burn of the sun against his flesh. There was something different about
my daddy. My mama kept shaking her head, placing emphasis on the
change since our arrival.

Daddy put on one of the suits that he purchased for his new job. He
moved slow due to the aftermath of the stroke, but his will to teach a
lesson demanded effort beyond what felt comfortable. He looked like a
Baptist preacher prepared to go to church on Easter Sunday. His movement and determination appeared as a lesson about the power of
resurrection. My coming home stirred new life in my daddy's body.
That's what my mama said as we waited for him to prepared to take us
to dinner.

"I'm taking you to G&D," he said.

G&D was my daddy's favorite steak house. I Didn't mention that
Glenda and I didn't eat red meat. Pleasing him meant more than our
dietary restrictions.

"You drive son," my daddy ordered. Glenda sat in the middle. My daddy sat near the window in his Ford F-150 truck. I started the truck and prepared to make my way to G&D. My daddy spoke before I pulled the gear down to the D to drive away from under the trees.

"How many miles I got on this truck," daddy asked.

I looked at the mileage. It was less than 6,000. I told him.

"A few years back, I went looking for a truck," he started with the lesson. "I ended up at Joe Machen's Ford. I only drive Fords."

If it's not a Ford, in my daddy's mind, it's a piece of junk.

"I found the truck I wanted and went back home. I waited a year before going back. When I got there, a salesman came out to ask what I wanted. I pointed at the truck I wanted. I told him to take that truck back for detail and I would be back tomorrow to pick it up. He asked how I would pay. I told him I'm making one payment."

I expected a lesson about saving money and not going into debt. My daddy was born in 1936. He experienced the pain after the Great Depression and knew the important lesson regarding waste not, want not. His race, combined with his philosophy on spending, prevented him from moving on up to a bigger house on the other side of the redline district. This was a lesson I knew well from his previous teachings.

"I came back the next day. My truck was where it was the day before. I asked the salesman why he didn't do what I said. He told me we didn't handle financing. I told him I had one payment. I pulled out my cashier check."

My daddy spoke with pride, but that wasn't the lesson.

"I told him to get my truck ready. They did. I rode my truck all day. I always wanted a new truck. I brought it home and parked it right here.

There was a long pause.

"The next day I had a stroke. I had another the next week. I ended up in the hospital. This is my first time in this truck since that day," my daddy took a long pause. He looked at me. Then he looked at Glenda.

"Don't wait for tomorrow when you see something you want. You never know what tomorrow brings."

Silence followed in respect of the lesson.

"Let's go eat."

It could be that daddy was telling me not to let a good woman get away. Maybe he was apologizing for the former lessons about saving money in preparation for a rainy day. My problem involved there being more rainy days than those with clear skies. It was hard raising three children while studying for degrees aimed at paving the way for better days. Maybe my daddy was teaching me a lesson about balance.

It was a lesson about not waiting too long to pursue the things you want in life. Be it a nice truck or a good woman, you never know what will come after a long drive on Tuesday. Wednesday may take the joy away. You never know what tomorrow brings. Don't wait too long, son.

It was the lesson my daddy gave me before I returned home to become his caregiver. My daddy's death has given me new perspective involving the lesson. Maybe my daddy was giving me a glimpse into what would come. Maybe the lesson was about the unfinished business between the two of us. There was father and son stuff left undone due to my relocation to North Carolina. There was bonding that needed to take place before it was too late. Maybe my daddy was challenging me to not wait until tomorrow to come back home to spend time with him. To learn more from one another before it's too late. Maybe my daddy put on a suit to show me the side I missed while I was away. I wasn't the only man wearing a suit. I wasn't the only one in need of something I couldn't gain on my own.

Like my daddy, I'd been saving for things like that truck. While saving for the things I desired, I could have taken advantage long before sickness came to rob me of more special moments.

Yeah, I like to think that was my daddy's lesson.

There's a more important lesson. It's one about assumptions. There was a time I assumed my daddy was too old fashioned to teach me lessons. Getting older has taught me young people think I'm too old to be "woke". It's painful when young folks believe you're too old to understand what is needed. I suppose each generation contends with old people being outdated and young people being too engrossed in their assumptions to listen.

15

ANOTHER GOOD DAY

D ays come and go. The significance of days become clouded by each seeming to be the same. They're not the same, but the blessing is the same.

Days are promises formed in our dreams. The sun rises each morning with the promise of a new day – another chance to embrace the beauty of God's creation. Each day ends with the sunset, and the rising of a moon that constantly changes to reflect the worlds beauty. Sameness is mingled with change to prevent taking life for granted. Everything seems the same, but there is massive distinction in what feels the same.

My daddy loved fishing. Fishing was his way to connect the pieces of life broken by the time between more than enough strength to run and not enough to stand on your own. Fishing was a burden now. It took more time to prepare to make the trip to McBaine, Missouri where my daddy did most of his fishing. It was a spot close to the Missouri River. There was plenty of catfish, perch and carp to be caught in the river.

"My grandmother told me the story of watching Abe walk up that hill," my daddy told me one day. "She was working in the field when he stepped off a boat on the Missouri River."

I image my great-grandmother thought Abe was Moses preparing to tell Pharaoh to let his people go. There's no doubt my daddy connected his grandmother's story to his own deliverance. He would have been a slave working in that same field if not for Abe starting a war to set the captives free.

My daddy never talked about how he felt about hearing my great-grandmother's story. It was the type of statement that didn't require commentary. It was enough knowing she saw Abe that day. It placed my daddy's life within an historical context. My daddy was born 72 years after the end of the Civil War.

"It could have been me" comes to mind when you hear grandma talking about working in the field when Abe made his way to the hotel on top of the hill.

I think a lot about what type of slave I would have been if not for Abe crafting the Emancipation Proclamation. While my daddy carried the skills of a man capable of maneuvering around the expectations of a slaveowner, words evoking thoughts of submission is difficult for me to fathom. No man is my master – I say. "Before I'd be a slave, I'd be buried in my grave and go home to my Lord and be free" – I say. I'd runaway before enduring the humiliation of slavery – I say. I'd fight back and stir a revolution – I say, but would I?

My judgment of my great-grandmother's and great-grandfather's compliance is based on things I will never fully understand. Both had seen and heard things that happened before I benefited from freedom. The short time between my great-grandmother's witness of a tall white man walking up a hill, and my walking up stairs to receive my college diploma, were filled with reminders of consequence.

They forgot more than I've seen. Their experiences involving race and racism conditioned them to act and speak in ways I'm incapable of fully understanding. There are lessons in those stories that I will never hear. They are too painful to be told to those who lack the will to stand in the heat of disappointment.

Disappointment is an intense word. There's more to it than the emotions we carry when a girl breaks our heart, or you receive notice that the job went to another person. Disappointment is about the stuff we can't fix. It's about waking up, day after day, to face a realty that refuses to go away.

Disappointment is about things stirred by a legion of past mistakes.

It's about eating the wrong foods for a long time and enduring the aftermath of diabetes. Disappointment is being reduced to walking with a cane or walker and taking multiple pills three times each day because you lack the insight to fight against the troubles brewing in your body.

Disappointment is the loss of youth and contending with the things we've taken for granted. Things like the freedom to move and the people who travelled to the other side to keep company with the Lord. Things like cooking your own meals and waking up every morning without the love of your life there to kiss and hug you tight. Disappointment is the memory of what used to be before everything changed.

I remember fishing with my daddy at the pond near where my great-grandmother saw Abe walk up that hill. My daddy didn't believe in talking while fishing. The fish can hear you. We would sit with multiple fishing poles. Mine was shorter than my daddy's because I was too small to manage the poles used by grown folks.

We sit in my daddy's boat all day. Sometimes the fish took the bait and we'd catch enough fish for ourselves and another family. My daddy was good at taking care of other people. I believe he enjoyed giving fish away just as much as cleaning and cooking the fish with a side of his potato salad, coleslaw and cornbread.

Fishing was part work and part family reunion. It was my daddy's way of spending time with his only son while giving back to others who lived in our neighborhood. Back in those days, sharing was part of what it meant to be black in a community where sharing cups of sugar, eggs and produce from the garden is how we all survived. Daddy set a picnic table in the back yard near the barbeque grill he made from an old steel drum. Cooking was my daddy's love language and the members of the Warrick ad Kenney family loved it when he spoke.

The silence when we fished kept me from the conversations I wanted to have with my daddy. I wanted to talk about baseball and music. Lou Brock was stealing bases for the St. Louis Cardinals and it looked like he was going to break the single season record. It looked like the Cardinals might win the pennant and Bob Gibson is the best pitcher in the league. We never talked about Aretha Franklin singing

R-E-S-P-E-C-T or the moves the Temptations made when they sang. "My Girl". Daddy loved music, but the fish might be listening.

The silence was interrupted with celebration whenever I caught a fish. Daddy's smile reminded me of a love deeper than talk about baseball and soul music. I wondered if this was the same spot where my grandfather taught my daddy to fish. Maybe my great-grandfather taught my grandfather, and it goes back to fathers and sons passing on a tradition long before Abe Lincoln walked up that hill.

On that day, shortly after returning home to be my daddy's caregiver, I learned a lesson about fishing. It was a lesson about the disappointment of things lost and the things we take for granted after all of it is taken away.

"I remember the days after the first stroke," my daddy began the lesson. "It was hard for me to walk. It was hard moving. The hardest part is I couldn't go fishing."

Fishing was taken away. My daddy gave his boat to his cousin along with his collection of fishing rods and the truck he drove to tow his boat. The smell of his special bait – a combination of wheat germ, cantaloupe, honey and God only knows what else – no longer reeked throughout the house on Saturday mornings just before Daddy made his way to the truck to go fishing.

Fishing was only a memory.

"One day, I woke up and my body felt different. I could move like I did before the stroke. Everything was perfect again," Daddy continued. "I called my brother Stanley and asked him if he wanted to go fishing. We drove down to McBaine to the spot where we always fish. I got out of the truck like I always do. We walked to our spot. Caught five fish. Laughed on the way back to the truck and talked about how good a day it was. It was like it was before the stroke."

Daddy took a long pause as he looked out the window while sitting in his blue, lazy boy chair. His long gaze outside gave the impression there was something there that caught his attention. I saw his Ford F-150 truck parked on the street and the two oak trees next to the driveway to captivate his attention. He was looking somewhere beyond the truck and trees. It wasn't the leaves stacked on the lawn or the wind that forced more leaves to the ground.

It was the memory.

"I woke up the next day and I was back to where I was before that day. I couldn't move. My body hurt like it did before that day."

More silence as my daddy looked in the direction of nowhere.

"I asked God why he did that to me. Why let me enjoy one day and take me back to what it was like before that day."

I thought about the question. I had no answer. I expected my daddy to talk about his rage. I expected to hear more about being mad at God for taking him back to the agony he felt before that one good day.

"God told me it's because he wanted me to remember the good days. God gave me a day to remember how much I love fishing. I got one more good day to help me through the rest."

I listened with more questions – but, why, I mean – my daddy stopped me in the middle of my thinking.

"Sometimes all we need is one good day to remember God's blessings. We think we need more than that, but one good day is all we need. It's enough to give us the strength to make it through the other days." I listened and embraced my lesson.

"Son don't waste too much time thinking about the bad days. You've been given some good days. Thank God. It's enough."

16

ASSUMPTIONS ABOUT RELIGION

I 've been thinking long and hard about how the theology of older black people has developed over the years. The common interpretation is to place it all within a context that views it as part of a system to manipulate black people into accepting slavery. The most troubling aspect of talk about black religious practice is the fact that slaves were forced into embracing the religious views of the people who kept them in slavery. They were stripped of their freedom, banished from the land of their birth and given a language and religion unlike what they knew.

The questions we face today reflect the relevance of maintaining a faith forced on our ancestors. Is Christianity a valid religion for those seeking harmony with their ancestors? There is no easy way for a Christian to come out with a positive answer without negating the credibility of arguments the critics of Christianity make. What does a Christian say in the face of facts that justify the rage of those who dismiss Christianity?

As a theologian and minister, I point to the work of people like the late James Cone, Gayraud Wilmore, Al Raboteau, Katie Canon and Jacquelyn Grant. The work of black liberation and womanist theologies helps recast of how we think about the message of Jesus. If God is God of the oppressed, as Cone argues in his book <u>Black</u>

Theology and Black Power (1969), we are granted the tools to talk
about God in ways that disproves the notions of white evangelical
Christianity. The problem isn't about Christianity as much as it is in
how white American Christians have historically interpreted Christianity as a tactic in the ongoing coercion of black people
and women.

My daddy's comments struck a chord due to the way his theology
works in justifying his pain. At least that's how I perceive things. His
illness, in his mind, was constructed by God to teach a lesson. His
good day was given to prove God's love in his continuing quest to
survive the consequence of lost activity. The good day is a blessing. My
daddy didn't ask why God could extend the joy of the one good day.
That day was enough to undo the pain of the other days. For me, I
need a more profound talk with Jesus.

My daddy's story was about his survival skills. It's the rationaliza-
tion he needed to move forward in ways that granted him the joy that
the world can't take away. It was his answer to God's continued presence in the pain. God didn't leave him alone to contend with the
inability to go fishing. He was given one more good day as a reminder
of the other days. For me, I'm confused by the assumptions of his
conclusion.

It's taken me time to rest with my daddy's feelings. I had to give
myself permission to hear him better without judging the nuances of
his theological claims. I want to challenge his conception of God's role
in making him sick and making him better for one more day. I want to
dig much deeper to discuss the nature of evil while pondering the
theological implications related to disappointment. How about the
presence of evil within the institutions that force havoc on the weak?
Where is the evil in the medical profession? How do you really feel
about your illness? Do you perceive it as sin? If so, why? What is your
role in that sin? What could you, me and others, have done to prevent
this evil?

My daddy's answer is simple. God gave him one more good day.
My feelings related to my daddy's theology is a reminder of the vast
gap between older people and folks who attended college. In the
minds of many, attending divinity school strips black folks of the faith
that carried us through all those bad years. Learning lessons from

white people, in the opinion of some, is behind the massive disparities in black communities.

In other words, don't forget what the good Lord done for you.

"After that whole generation had been gathered to their ancestors, another generation grew up who knew neither the LORD nor what he had done for Israel," Judges 2:10 reads. My discussion with my daddy about his one good day left me wondering about my role in helping people forget the God who blessed black people before I attended college.

I took a trip to the river after my daddy's death. It was my way of connecting with my ancestors – the ones who fished at that spot. The ancestors who believed God controls all things, even the bad that comes in the middle of singing versus about the Lord making a way out of no way. I prayed for the spirit of my great-grandmother to come to me. I needed her to help me understand better, not in the great bye and bye, but right now. I needed her to show me the joy on this side of the river. Show me the faith that granted her the strength to overcome.

I desired the strength of the lessons taught long before black folks could read books on theology to help them comprehend why trouble comes to those who walk by faith.

There, by the riverside, the spirit of great grandma came to me. Her spirit stirred in me a deeper understanding of the faith of the slaves. Their faith was not about the "what if" of God. Their faith was intended to foster lessons regarding survival. Their faith was about being carried when you felt yourself falling and no one else is there to break your fall. Their faith was about being trapped within a cycle of disappointment with nothing but trouble in the way along with a bunch of tears. Their faith was about living with distress while hoping for a different life on the other side of the river.

The faith of my ancestors is not the same as the faith of the white people who used religion to force submission. Black folks cried for freedom. They wanted a better life for their children. My great-grandmother saw Abe Lincoln walk up that hill and prayed for the end of her troubles. My daddy was taught to embrace God's presence within the sorrow. God is still there. When we can't make it to the river, God gives us one more day.

My daddy's lesson was about a different type of faith. Mine is a faith stirred by the benefit of advanced theological training. Mine is a faith ripened in books my ancestors were not allowed to read. I've come to conclusions after musing over the scholarship of great black men and women. I've formed deductions with the witness of more than my ancestors knew. Their faith was based on nothing less than Jesus Christ and his righteousness. Mine is constructed from a place of deep learning, while their faith comes from a place deeper than the mind can digest – the faith planted in their hearts.

My daddy sat in his blue lazy boy chair. He looked at a place beyond his truck, the trees and leaves. He focused on a place on the other side of things we see, and found a faith grounded in the substance of things hoped for, rooted in things we can't see. He trusted in the message he heard the day after his good day.

The day is a gift.

There's no sorrow there. One day is all you need when God used it to remind my daddy it's enough to give you hope when you can't make your way back to the river.

17

LESSON ABOUT CHANGED IDENTITY

Time has a way of confusing the truth. When you're young, there's plenty of it to waste. When you're older, there's never enough to repair the mistakes. Time never stops. It's a constant buildup of memories that hide to truth. When the clock finally stops, life is measured by things undone and left behind.

When my daddy started shaking, it felt like everything stopped. The seizure started when he was eating scrambled eggs. The preparation of the eggs on his plate resembled the rapid motion of his body. I did what had become a common practice. I stood there too long given the situation. I didn't know what to do, and, if I had known, I'm not sure it would have made a difference.

I placed a hand on his chest and prayed for the shaking to stop. My prayer was answered shortly after I dialed 9-1-1. That part was easy. Picking up a phone and calling people who knew how to handle these types of situations seemed to define my work. I was a cook, watchman, nurse assistant and administrative assistant. None of it was enough when a shaking body is added to the list of unknowns that impact the quality of care.

It didn't take long for emergency medical services to arrive. It wasn't as cold as the last time and the streets weren't packed with snow. It wasn't a broken femur this time. There was something broken in my daddy's head. He wasn't responding like before. This time his body danced in the chair while his eyes gazed in the direction of a place far away – beyond things in this world. Something was wrong. It was different this time.

Time had taken a toll on my daddy's body. Time was fading faster than before. The pace of my heartbeat was much faster than before, and the time needed to process my feelings was denied because I felt time coming to an end. This time, it would be different. Time introduced the enemy of my faith. How many times could my daddy keep going back to the hospital and other places designed to grant him more time?

The doctors were confused by what was happening. It took a few days and numerous tests to determine it was an infection. It started with his ears and spread to his brain. The doctors didn't tell me the second part until later, but it didn't take much to know my daddy was taking a trip with a one-way ticket. I knew he wouldn't come back home this time. Not the same as before. This time would be different.

His visit to the rehabilitation center was different. The nurses and staff knew it, and they did their best to prepare me for what was coming.

"This reminds me of my father," the only male nurse on staff told me one day after noticing a few tears stuck on the corner of my eyes. "I'm been there."

He gave me a hug. It was one of those special moments when black men connect beyond words. We shared a common faith. He is a member of the male chorus at Second Baptist Church. Another black man who knows the joy of having a good daddy. His hug reminded me my daddy was in good hands. I felt it more than before.

They call it sun downing. I perceived it was dementia. It was bad most of the time, but it was worse at night. It was amplified by my daddy's struggles with hearing. He did his best to comprehend, but I could tell he was becoming more frustrated with questions he couldn't hear.

"I'm sorry baby," he often responded with a smile. "I can't hear a word you're saying."

He spent most of the night lying in bed starring at a place beyond what I could see. His nights were an escape beyond the trips back and forth to places designed to heal his body. My daddy appeared to be a man trapped by broken promises. Time had evaporated his dream of fishing down by the river and planting flowers in his garden. I would spend my nights watching my daddy look in the direction of those night shadows.

Visiting my daddy at the rehabilitation center got harder each day. I wondered about what my daddy was thinking. Was it about missing my mama who was too far away to visit every day? Was he thinking about Crystal, who died long ago after battling brain cancer? Or, was it about the promise he made to himself a long time ago?

"Son, all I ever wanted in life was to take care of my wife and children. That and a nice truck. That's all I ever wanted," it was my daddy's repeated lesson regarding the purpose of his life.

I thought a lot about my daddy's smile. He never complained. He never raised his voice during those days since I left Durham, North Carolina to become his caregiver. I wondered about how he felt about my being present to love him through the challenges he faced. More than all of that, I wondered if my daddy knew how much I love him, and how grateful I am to be raised by a daddy who made promises that involved loving me.

I found a parking space at the rehabilitation center. It felt like I was glued to the seat in the car I purchased for my daddy. The 2012 Lincoln MKZ was easier for my daddy to get in and out during his doctor appointments. I couldn't move because of the weight of the moment. I purchased the car for my daddy, and he hadn't seen it due to his health condition. I brought it because my daddy only purchases Ford's. I never asked him why. It didn't matter. I wanted my daddy to sit in the car purchased for his comfort.

"I brought this car to please you, Daddy," I whispered like my daddy was listening. "I did this for you."

The sun was going down. I knew what to expect inside.

My pain wouldn't let me move. I thought about things my daddy did to please others. The love for my mother. The gifts purchased for me and my sisters every Christmas. The furniture he gave me for my first apartment when I was only 18 and too stupid to know what I was doing. The Ford Pinto I wrecked and the Ford LTD he purchased after I wrecked the Pinto while playing with my girlfriend. I pondered all the lessons offered over the years, and how I refused to listen because, in my mind, my daddy was too old, and the way he thought was too old school to be applied to my new school ways.

I cried because I never did enough to say thank you. I cried because I never did enough to show my appreciation. I cried because I feared it was too late.

I looked at my watch. It was after 6:00 p.m. I had time to join my daddy for dinner. I walked through the doors like other days. It felt different. I turned left at the reception desk walked past the offices on my way to the elevator and pressed the G button. The door opened and opened again when I arrived on the ground floor.

Something felt different.

I turned right and walked through the double doors. My daddy wasn't sitting in the cafeteria, so I continued until I entered the community room. My daddy wasn't there. He rarely sat there with others watching television. I turned left at the nursing station.

Something felt different.

I walked to my daddy's room expecting him to be laying in his bed.

Something was different. My daddy was sitting in a chair. The light was on. The television was turned off. He was dressed in gray sweatpants with a matching top. He looked like he was ready to leave the rehabilitation center.

"I'm ready to go home," my daddy was crying.

"I know daddy."

"I'm tired. I'm ready to go home," his voice raised and quivered just enough to accent his conviction.

"I'm gonna take you home daddy. When you get better. I'll take you home."

"No," his body trembled. "I wanna go home. I wanna go home."

My daddy repeated his desire until his words matched the tears. My daddy was tired. Really tired. I knew what my daddy wanted. I wasn't prepared for what my daddy wanted.

"My daddy did the same thing," the male nurse who hugged me was standing behind me as if he knew I would need him soon. I looked back and saw two other nurses positioned to support me when my daddy's message settled in enough to make me weak." I needed them. I was weak.

"I want to go home. I want to go home," my daddy continued with his request as the nurses took care of me.

"He's tired. He's ready," the male nurse said.

"I know. I know. It's hard. It's hard to let him go."

Everything felt different for a reason. As much as the moment was about my daddy letting go of his desire to live, it was also about me preparing to accept my refusal to let go. The force of that moment wasn't fully felt until after my daddy took his last breath. The lesson required me to let go before finding the impact of its comfort.

The comfort came in a dream.

I dreamed of fishing with my daddy. It was a sunny day and the fish were biting. My daddy joked about there being too many fish for us to eat.

The dream shifted to my giving my daddy's eulogy. I spoke about my daddy's love for fishing. I talked about his love for his wife and children. I talked about his promise to me – all he wanted was to provide for his family. He promised to take care of me.

The dream felt real. I reached for pen and paper and wrote down the key points from the dream. I took a quick shower and prepared to get dressed. I had turned in my final grades for the class I taught at the University of Missouri. My plan was to head to the rehabilitation center and spend most of the day with my daddy.

My cell phone rang while I buttoned my shirt.

"Mr. Kenney, this is one of the nurses at the rehab center. Your father has coded. I need to know if you want us to resuscitate?"

"What?"

"Mr. Kenney, do you want us to resuscitate?" I couldn't answer. I couldn't think.

The nurse hung up. I didn't know what to say. I didn't know what to do.

I called Glenda. I called Glenda because she knows me. She knows my daddy. She has watched me cry. She has prayed with and for me. I called Glenda because I knew she would understand. I called Glenda because she buried her father on her birthday and cared for the love of her mother's life until his death. Glenda understood the hurt that comes with loving and caring for your daddy and the emotions that come when there is no more you can give.

"Glenda, they just called me to...," I told her the rest. I told her I didn't know what to say.

"Where are you," she asked.

"I'm headed to the rehab center," I responded. As we talked, I received a call from the same nurse who asked if I wanted to resuscitate.

"Mr. Kenney, your daddy has been sent to the hospital. You can meet him there."

I clicked back to the call with Glenda and gave her the news.

"You go there. I'll get back to you."

As I approached Boone County Hospital, I received another call informing me my daddy was transported to the University of Missouri Medical Center. His condition required he be sent there. I arrived less than 10 minutes later and parked in a space near the emergency room.

I was told they were working on my daddy. He coded twice since leaving the rehabilitation center.

I called Glenda to give updates.

"I'm on my way," I cried some more.

I called my mother and sister. I called my children. I called Cecil, my cousin who took care of my daddy before I came back home.

I remember begging God to send someone to support me while waiting for bad news. My daddy was moved to a room in intensive care and I was granted permission to see him. A doctor met me to prepare me for what I would see. My daddy was brain dead. His body was crowded with tubes attached to a variety of machines aimed at keeping him alive. My daddy's face was swollen like a man beaten by a combination of fist and other weapons. My daddy laid frozen like death already arrived to take his last breath.

I listened to every word the doctor uttered. There isn't much we can do. We will continue to try until there is nothing we can do. I heard every word.

The doctors were preparing me for the end. They were making sure I was able to accept the end.

It was time to let my daddy go. It was my task to prepare the rest of the family to find peace in letting him go.

All my life and my daddy's lessons fused in a moment of profound clarity. I contemplated the teachings since Crystals death – the ones about the meaning of death after countless prayers for healing. I considered my rage after prayers weren't answered. I blamed God and the teachings of the Church for failing to adequately prepare me for my sister's death. This time was different. The time between Crystal and daddy's comma prepared me for this battle to understand.

I embraced the teaching of professors like Harmon Smith and Willie Jennings who helped me find meaning in death. My lifetime grappling with death brought me to this new challenge in embracing all that comes with loving and letting a person be free to go home.

"I wanna go home," my daddy's final declaration before being draped in tubes, was a message meant to set me free.

My daddy didn't want this type of life. Going home was a statement of trust in a new possibility. Everything I preached, and claimed to believe, hinged on my faith in a better life for my daddy. That life for my daddy required embracing the beauty of death as an ongoing certainty of life.

My task was to prepare my family for the promises my daddy trusted before his death.

Glenda Jones and Janice Webster were parked in front of my daddy's house when I returned from the hospital. Betty Redwood was unable to make the trip. The three comprised the dance ministry at Compassion Ministries. I called them Carl's Angels out of respect for the love they have given over the years. They always showed up when I need support.

They checked in at a nearby hotel and began the challenge of preparing me for what would come next. Like Glenda, Janice witnessed the death of her father. They knew the trials of caregiving firsthand. Both continue to serve mothers while doing their best to maintain enough balance to prevent mental collapse. They understand the guilt that comes with not being able to give enough. They know the pain related to needing time away from it all.

Glenda and Janice refused to allow me to experience what was coming alone. Other faithful members of Compassion Ministries, the congregation I served before leaving Durham, and Orange Grove Missionary Baptist Church, the congregation I led as senior pastor before planting Compassion Ministries, called to support me. The members at Bethel Church rose to the occasion in ways I will never forget.

My mother, sister, nephew and Stanley, my daddy's brother, arrived on Saturday. I found it critical that everyone have a chance to say goodbye before my daddy took his last breath. We took turns in pairs watching my daddy survive through the aide of the life support system. I found solace that no one commented on God's ability to fix it. I was clear that my daddy's healing would come in his death. His own words were a challenge to me to do the right thing when the time came to say goodbye.

"I'm ready to go home."

My mama didn't say much. Sandra spent most of her time holding me and crying. My nephew did his best to support his grandmother and mother while Glenda and Janice watched his three daughters. Cecil did what he had done alone – standing with my daddy the best he could. My uncle did his best to be strong. I discerned he was weak.

I thought long and hard about the death of Cecil's father. His funeral was held a week after I arrived home to take care of my daddy. Cecil, Sr was like a daddy to me. Cecil Jr., Gregory, Debbie, Dianne and Dalphine were like brothers and sisters. Cecil Jr's presence at my daddy's bedside reminded me of another truth. It felt like everyone was dying.

George "Doodle Bug" Crum and Darron "Cornbread" Crum, my cousins and close friends growing up, died the same year. Herbert "Pee Wee", my daddy's cousin and Darron's father, died shortly after my daddy. Sickness and death surrounded me in a way that left me believing my purpose in returning home was to bury the dead.

A part of my past was dying with my daddy. As I made my way to visit my daddy at the hospital, I received word that Lonnie Ratliff was dying. Lonnie was another man like my daddy who lived in my neighborhood. Mary Ratliff, his wife, was the State President for the NAACP. Pam and Deborah, their daughters, and Kenneth, their son, lived less than 50 yards from where we lived. Kenneth was the little brother I craved growing up. Word of his death reached me years after it happened.

I was surrounded by thoughts of death.

There was the thought of people who died while I was away. There was the thought of people who died before I had a chance to say good-bye. I never told "Doodle Bug" goodbye. I wasn't there to support my cousins and friends during their last days. Some struggled with terminal illness. All of them shaped my life.

I had to preach that Sunday. It was Pentecost Sunday, May 24, 2015. I preached from Acts 2:1-21. I remember leaning heavily on Ezekiel 37:1-14 in guiding me spiritually through the week. I kept asking, "can these dry bones live?"

Like the scripture stated, the situation we faced was an unlikely scene of a valley filled with "very dry" bones. The very dry removed all doubt as to the presence of life in this desolate place. There was no life. There was no hope for those listening to the prophet's message. I preached from a valley that day.

I sought hope in the valley. All of it appeared as a pile of bones that formed a barricade of desolation. The bones covered the possibility for new life. The text challenged me to claim a faith beyond the presence of bones. Could these bones live? Could my daddy's withering bones receive a new body enlivened by the breath of life that is the Spirit of God? Is there hope in the presence of this hopeless scenario?

Could God show up after I left church to say goodbye to my daddy? My own bones felt dry – very dry – and I prayed for the breath of new life to resurrect my withering faith. I leaned on Ezekiel's prophesy to inspire my hope in a reasonable expectation for help.

As much as I needed a revived spirit, I didn't preach the text from Ezekiel. I preached from Acts because I felt it was what the congregation needed. I tussled with the need to preach myself beyond the pain versus fulfilling my obligation to the congregation. This was another moment that brought to bear the confusion I carried related to cultural difference in preaching to a mostly white congregation. I assumed the congregation needed a message about the meaning and significance of Pentecost given the state of race relations in the city, nation and world.

There is no doubt that my placement at Bethel Church provided a unique opportunity to delve into issues that help frame with it means to be the Church

Universal. The Day of Pentecost is about the unveiling of the Holy Spirit as the ongoing work of the Spirit of Jesus. It's about naming those present that day, and how the barriers of race, language and culture is offset by the Spirit's will in aiding people in understanding those who spoke different languages. The day is about overcoming the curse of Babel by reversing what kept us from seeing one another beyond our differences.

Yes, there was, on that day, a need for the black co-pastor of a mostly white congregation to announce the end of division. But there was also a need for me to receive what I needed. Who would preach the word from God that I needed – if not me?

I needed to say my faith is damaged by the presence of consuming death. These bones are piled up too high for me to see the glory on the other side of death. I needed to announce my pain before the people. My daddy is dying. People I've known are dying. Many have already died. Where is God in this consuming valley of dry bones?

Beyond the message I needed to preach for comfort in my time of need, I needed the idiomatic expression of the black faith tradition. I needed to shout it out in a way that evokes the celebration found within the black church. This was a moment to declare "weeping may endure for a night, but joy comes in the morning". This was time to call on the mighty clouds of witnesses who understand the culture and context of black worship.

The people present that day lacked the cultural capacity in helping me shout my pain out. It would have confused them if I exposed them to what it means when a black preacher uses the text to dig from under the valley of dry bones. I needed a congregation willing to allow me to go there without creating space for an extension of cultural differences.

Glenda and Janice were there to witness the moment. My mama, sister and nephew witnessed my preaching that day. They needed what I needed that day, but the culture of the congregation complicated my ability to match the spirit of black church worship in a context far removed from what that means. In experiencing my daddy's impending death, I discovered something that was missing in preparing me for this moment – the life of the black church.

We headed to the hospital immediately after worship. I knew what was coming, but I'm not sure the others knew. It was time to say goodbye.

We gathered around my daddy's body waiting for the doctor to arrive. There was nothing else we could do. As we waited, a Chaplain arrived to offer last rights prayer. I stood infuriated by her presence. She entered our space uninvited. She prayed without asking what we knew. She failed to honor the families right in letting my daddy go before asking for the prayer.

My desire to address the issue faded after I pondered my place in the moment. It was my role to serve as my family's priest. It was my role to take them through a process that helped them in letting my daddy go. Although they hadn't spoken to the doctor, I knew the severity of the moment. I knew it was over. The prayer offered by the hospital Chaplin had to be minimized given what I had to do next.

My grievance with the Chaplin remains. In dealing with families during decisions involving death, never assume the family is aware of why you are present. It's clear a member of the medical staff called for a Chaplin, but that doesn't give the Chaplin the right to offer last rites without the family's permission.

The doctor arrived shortly after the Chaplin departed. He shared the extent of my daddy's condition. He was brain dead, and there was nothing they could do. I asked the doctor to give us time to say goodbye before pulling the plug. We joined hands. Glenda and Janice held my hands. My mama, my uncle Stanley, my sister, my nephew and my cousin were in the room. I told everyone to say goodbye.

My mama told my daddy she loved him, he is a good husband and she is grateful.

Sandra told my daddy she loved him. She cried bitterly. My nephew did the same and Cecil spoke like a son. My uncle struggled to find words that matched his emotions. Glenda and Janice thanked my daddy for all he did in being a good father and husband. Glenda talked about her feelings related to conversations they had back when we visited in 2002.

I thanked my daddy for fulfilling his promise. He taught me how to be a man. I promised to remember his teachings. When I finished thanking my daddy, I prayed.

The peace of God was in the room.

The doctor returned to remove the tubes. It didn't take long. My daddy took his last breath. I closed my eyes and allowed the tears to come. I missed him already, but I was so thankful my daddy had entered his perfect peace.

There's the fulfillment of a sacred promises in death. I'm connected to my daddy by the cross we carried together during my caregiving. My caregiving was more than a gift to my daddy. It's my daddy's gift to me. In dying, I received part of my daddy's spirit. His lifetime of promises infused his spirit and memory in me. More than ever, my daddy lives in and through me as a result of his promises.

My daddy's promises are to mold me into a man who honors his life and faith. Into my heart my daddy departed his spirit. My challenge is in offering his spirit to my son and daughters. Like my daddy, my desire is to love and support my children. Prayerfully, there will be a wife to love like my daddy loved my mama. My daddy left me with teachings that help me become a man worthy of being a husband.

18

REFLECTIONS AFTER DADDY'S DEATH

The gushes of tears continue to find me. I carry the burden of missing my father. That will never change. What is the lesson? I embrace and love my tears.

I wonder about those who lack the resources to do what I did for my daddy. What about those without proper insurance to pay the cost to die with dignity? What about those trapped in the battle over Medicaid expansion in states controlled by insensitive legislators?

Caregiving is made easier when there is money to pay the bills. The cost for funerals forces some families to pay more than they can afford. It's easy to get trapped into correlating the cost of a funeral with how much you love the deceased. Social media is bursting with Go Fund me pages to pay the funeral expenses. The cost to bury the dead leaves many families lingering in chaos after the last breath.

My daddy took care to assure most of the cost for his funeral was covered before he died. In addition to sharing the details for his funeral, my daddy made sure I knew the expenses for my mama's funeral was paid. My daddy died freeing me of the burden of collecting money from family and friends.

I was free to grieve and heal.

This point can't be overstated. It is a critical distinction among black and white families. The privilege of being white often involves the inheritance left to family members. The passing of generational wealth assists in the healing of family members after death. Many black families spend the days leading up to the funeral trapped in processing the cost to bury when they should be engaged in the work of healing.

My daddy's gift is in releasing me from the brutal task of fundraising for his funeral. I was free to reflect on how my daddy must have felt having his only son wash urine off his body. I spent the days before the funeral pondering the grueling work of caregiving. I contemplated the emotional and physical toil of caregiving and the time it would take for me to overcome the experience. Caregiving beats the soul with a fury that demands constant review regarding why one does it, and how they survive each day. It's an emotional rollercoaster that leaves you ecstatic for taking the journey while leaving you empty when it's over.

No one told me about the days after the last breath.

There are few days absent of tears because I miss him so much. They come when I least expect them. They consume my moments with a memory that makes it hard not to cry. I've cried while reaching for catfish at the grocery store. The memory of our disagreement makes me smile. I told him catfish are rats that live in the river. He responded, "boy, you don't know what you're missing."

The tears flow while I'm driving in the car, I purchased for him. My wish for him were rides to McBaine and Rocheport – the places where he lived growing up in mid-Missouri. I hoped the drives to the places of his childhood memories would stir more conversations about life before he married my mama and the two of them conceived me.

I never got the chance to take daddy on a ride down by the river. That is where we used to fish when I was too young to understand that daddy would someday leave me to go to a place beyond human misery. I admired his strength and the silence that said more than words can utter when a father and son are fishing.

The tears come when I hear Sam Cooke singing "A Change is Gonna Come". His love for music is one of the many things lodged in my DNA. The tears increase when I think of King, my son, who's life, like my father and me, is inspired and shaped by the music we all love.

I'll never forget his last breath.

Nothing in my life has impacted me more than my father's death. The past years have left me pondering the veiled meanings of the messages my daddy gave me before he said goodbye. I'm left craving more of his wisdom concealed in stories about growing up with old-fashioned ways. His strength was in his passion to love beyond differences.

My daddy's death left a void affected by things I couldn't fix before he died. My will to make things better made it hard to say, "see you later". The unabashed tears of his final days disturbed my desire to fulfill all that was missing. My yearning to make things better served as my payback for all the things he had done for me.

All I wanted was to give him more. The thoughts of things taken away kept me stuck in the longing to restore what was lost. What could have been if his hand hadn't been damaged by a gun shot when he was 19 years-old? Would he have become the champion boxer or artist that many believed was his destiny?

My dream for my daddy was for him to see the world his son has seen. I imagined the smile upon witnessing the blue water in Jamaica. I wanted to watch him casting rods for big fish in the ocean. I wanted to take him on a safari in Zimbabwe and to the Louvre in Paris to give him a chance to see the things he watched on television.

I wanted to take him to football games and boxing matches. More than anything, I wanted his last days to free him from the limits of the place he called home.

I came home to rescue my father from the limits caused by sickness. Years later, I'm trapped in the thought that I failed him. His sickness was more powerful than my will to set my daddy free. Deep down, I know none of that is true. I did my best and my daddy appreciated our days together. Knowing the truth isn't enough to counter the guilt stirred by my unfulfilled dream – days by the riverside.

These are the gifts of caregiving. Those tasked with providing for their parents, or other family members, begin with the assumption that they do it for them. They begin hoping to rescue their loved ones from the misery they perceive as the locked door. They begin with the will to unlock the door that will set their loved ones free to explore all that has been missing.

For me, it took time after death to understand the real purpose of caregiving. The gift isn't in overcoming what the caretaker is missing. The gift is unlocking the doors to explore all assumptions. Those assumptions robbed me of the experience of knowing and loving my daddy beyond my sense of reality. Overcoming assumptions paves the way to greater understanding among people separated from the heartbeat of their loved ones.

It takes time to find yourself after caregiving ends with death. Part of the lesson is in learning how to live again. After giving so much of yourself, it takes time to accept the love received beyond your giving. It takes time to accept more has been gained than was lost along the way.

I've learned to embrace the tears. My daddy is there to remind me of what I was missing before I came back home. My daddy didn't need me to help him escape his misery. My daddy was there to teach me lessons imparted while in the presence of a person who loves me more than I could understand.

It's the hardest thing I've ever done. It's the most rewarding thing I've ever done. What appears as two contradictory statements is the best way to relate the emotions associated with caregiving. For those who have been there and done that, these are the words that stir tears accompanied with nodding heads.

19

FISHING ON THE OTHER SIDE

P reparing for a funeral is a massive distraction. It takes focus away from the flood of tears waiting to erupt as soon as you take time to rest. My daddy took care of most of the hard work. Daddy purchased the casket and gravesite as soon as he started thinking about death. He often reminded me of the details – the name of the funeral home, the amount in his insurance policy – while informing me he also took care of my mama's burial expenses. My daddy took pride in being prepared for the end. He buried enough people in his lifetime to know the burden placed on those left behind.

I was surrounded by a team of amazing friends who made sure my daddy's funeral was managed the right way. Reverend Muriel Johnson, Reverend Bonnie Cassida, Reverend Clanton C.W. Dawson, Jr., Reverend Cassandra Gould, Deborah Dalton, Traci Kleekamp-Wilson and the members at Bethel Church rose to the occasion. The meal after the funeral was prepared by a group of black women who tutored the members at Bethel Church on the culture of feeding black people. Deborah Dalton created the perfect program with pictures printed in color.

A picture of my father looking cool while walking in snow is on the cover. The words, "Carl W. Kenney, Sr., November 7, 1936 – May 24, 2015" appear under the picture. The funeral was held on May 30, 2015 at Bethel Church – a reminder that Progressive Missionary Baptist Church, my daddy's church home, demanded payment to have the funeral service there. It hurt knowing the church next to my daddy's house – the one where my baby sister joined before she died, where my grandfather was eulogized and where I preached my first sermon – wasn't available to lift fond memories of my daddy.

Another cool picture of my daddy appears on the top of the left-fold inside page. He was sitting outside, surrounded by nature, with sunglasses covering his eyes. Look at that smile. I imagined his love for all things outside made him feel at home.

The first line of the obituary reads, "Carl W. Kenney, Sr. loved fishing, hunting and took pride in watching plants grow in his garden. He was known for having a sense of humor and a smile that lured people in within seconds of the first hello."

A picture of the family is on the bottom of the middle-fold inside page. A younger me with an afro wearing a denim jump suit, made by my mother, and blue blazer stood behind my daddy and next to Sandra. I was 18 years-old at the time the picture was taken. I wondered if my parents knew the gold necklace around my neck was a marijuana leaf. Sandra had a smile that evoked memories of better days. My daddy and mama were both smiling. I was the only one not smiling.

The picture on the top of the right-fold inside page is my father receiving a plaque from Shelter Insurance Company. A.D. Sappington, the former president at Shelter Insurance Company, is shaking my daddy's hand in celebration of 25 years of service. Sappington, the man who handed a man a check to pay for my daddy's house, considered my daddy a friend. At least that's how my daddy felt.

YEARS AFTER SAPPINGTON'S DEATH, my daddy received a call from Sappington's daughter out of concern for her mother. My daddy made his way to the house, rang the doorbell and broke in after no one answered the door. He found Mrs. Sappington dead. My daddy's connection with Shelter Insurance Company and the Sappington family is best understood in the context of my daddy's smile. People loved him. He deserved their love.

My uncle Stanley was at the funeral to say goodbye. He's the last remaining sibling. Uncle James and my aunts – Elizabeth, Nokomis and Corine – died years ago. Uncle Cecil, Nokomis's husband, was gone. Uncle Herman and Uncle Charles were there to say goodbye along with aunt Joy, Uncle James' widow. Cousins I hadn't seen in years were there. Both sides of the family, the Warrick's and Kenney's showed up to remember my daddy.

It was raining outside. Deacon Harold Warren talked about his relationship with my daddy.. I took it all in because I knew every word was true. A few members from Quinn Chapel AME Church prepared to sing before the eulogy. Then it happened. Reverend Gould, the pastor at Quinn Chapel, approached me. Muriel Johnson, the regional associate minister of the American Baptist Churches of the Great Rivers Region, stood next to her holding my robe. They reached out for me to follow them.

We walked down the center aisle, symbolizing a change in me. I left the sanctuary as the son of Carl W. Kenney, Sr. I would return as the minister appointed to speak that day. It was a powerful statement that caught many in the room off guard. Each step reminded me of the journey to that moment. My steps growing up. My steps falling apart. My steps being picked up by my daddy. Being loved by my daddy. Supported by him, sometimes in his silence, in ways that make me a better man.

Muriel removed my jacket. They placed the robe on me. They prayed for me in that way that reflects the witness of black women. They stood in the proverbial gap with me. While praying, I reflected on Cassandra's story. He mother died while she was being appointed by the African Methodist Episcopal Church to serve Quinn Chapel AME Church. She eulogized her mother before taking her place as pastor. She knows the pain related to burying a parent. She understands how it feels to stand between roles as a hurting child and a servant of God.

We marched back down the center aisle. This time, I'm cloaked in liturgical garment. It's a robe designed by and made by my mother. The African mud cloth made a statement regarding my witness as a black preacher/prophet. I was standing in the place I was called to serve. I did so as a black son of a black father who endured those many trails and struggles associated with black life in America.

I stood in a place surrounded by black and white people. Some of them knew my daddy. Some of them only know my work as the co-pastor of their church. Some know the drain of living while black. They know what it meant for my daddy to work hard to support his wife and children within the bitter racism of the 1950's until his death. Some know what my daddy was denied. Many knew my daddy's smile, but they didn't know the courage and faith it took to keep smiling when life is an endless struggle.

I stood before the people with my daddy in front of me in a coffin. What did it all mean? Why here? Why now? Why me?

What is the meaning behind giving this eulogy here? Is this a statement about my daddy's life or is it a reflection of his home church refusing to allow him to be celebrated there because he hadn't been to church and paid his tithes? Is there a message for all of us?

There is.

This is the community my daddy loved. My daddy lived to love all people. He never talked about race. I did. I did a lot. I felt the burden of racism, but my daddy had a will for a world not troubled by race and racism. My standing in the pulpit at Bethel Church was a statement about my daddy, but it was also a statement about how my work and life is connected to the lessons and promises of my daddy.

My daddy willed this moment for me. I felt the energy of my daddy's life. This was my daddy's promise.

I heard my daddy speak to me.

"You can go anywhere. You can do anything. There is nothing you can't achieve. My desire for you has always been that you live beyond the limits."

My daddy didn't teach me how to preach. My daddy didn't inspire my will to write. Being a journalist, author, preacher, teacher – none of it – is a direct reflection of what my daddy inspired. Yet, all of it is a manifestation of how my daddy lived. My being in that space, standing before white and black people to eulogize my daddy, was a celebration of my daddy's unwillingness to be defined by his race.

My daddy's promise was to give me strength, courage, faith, hope and an uncompromised gratitude for the things that matter most in life. He gave me a love for family and a will to make everyone I meet my best friend. My daddy taught me to never measure people based on what you see. There is good in all of us.

Standing there, in my African liturgical robe, was the eulogy. I'm my daddy's eulogy because I am the expression of my daddy's promise.

"Tell my story son," I felt my daddy speak.

All of it was in preparation for that moment. All of it. My coming back home was to help me understand the promise. Taking care of my daddy was to open my eyes to what I was unwilling to see. I've been broken for this moment. I've been stripped of my pride and denied certain privileges to shape me beyond my assumptions. I had to cry more to feel it beyond the stuff I wanted to deny. I had to fight against myself to embrace my daddy's contribution in making me a better man. I did not get here by myself. My daddy shaped every part of me. Everyday. Even when I assumed it was all about me. I took a bunch of deep breaths.

"My mama made this robe," I began. "My mama is a part of me."

I talked about my daddy's promise to his wife and children. I noticed the nods in the room.

I talked about how hard my daddy worked to provide for his family. More nods.

I talked about how much my daddy loved fishing. I told the story about my daddy having one last good day after suffering a stroke. He went fishing that day, came home and was sick again the next day.

I told them about the dream of my daddy fishing somewhere on the other side of death.

I talked about my daddy's last request. He wanted to go home. He was tired. He's home now.

The emotions were too much to carry. The tears were coming, and I couldn't say much more. The tears weren't about missing my daddy. These tears felt like a thank you letter for all the unspoken promises offered through the years.

The long drive to the gravesite helped us heal. My mama and sister didn't say much. King and Krista were there to tell granddaddy good-bye. Lenise wasn't able to make it in time for the funeral. My desire to teach my children my daddy's lessons overwhelmed me. I wanted to tell them my daddy is with us. There was no need. We felt my daddy's presence. I suppose that's one of his promises.

I'm not going far. Just taking a break to go fishing.

Call when you need me.

I need you daddy. I always will.

20

THE LESSON IN THE DOING

My being a caregiver wasn't new. My attempt to manage numerous tasks were an extension of the life I chose long before becoming my daddy's caregiver. Caregiving exposed truths about strengths and weaknesses that re-shaped life. It is my strength that gave me the will to take on the responsibility of being my daddy's caregiver. It was my weakness in failing to honor my personal needs that helped me say yes. What appears as a strength is, in part, rooted in weakness. What appears as a weakness is based on a deeper strength.

Owning and naming both strengths and weaknesses are critical in overcoming the brokenness after the need for caregiving ends. The days after death, in many ways, are harder than the time spent in taking care of another person. The aftermath is about the lessons, and some are hard to embrace due to the guilt and shame that makes it difficult to face the truth. Things die beyond the person placed in the grave. The aftershock of caregiving is facing our own emotional and spiritual death.

Acknowledging wounds that result in death seem wrong due to the focus on personal pain. Guilt makes it challenging to accept how caregiving leaves you damaged. We're taught to celebrate martyrdom. Dying for others is the work of the crucified Christ – we're told. We perceive caregiving as a witness of authentic faith, leaving us burdened by the death that results from taking on that responsibility. It's easier to revel in benefits of caregiving than sharing the pain that comes with sacrificing for the person you love.

It is the hardest thing a person will do.

For me, and many others, the lessons renew the load of caregiving. The days, months and years, after my daddy died, came with lessons that made it difficult to return to my life before deciding to take on the responsibility.

What are the lessons?

Lesson #1. I decided to become my daddy's caregiver because I needed it as much as he needed me. Choosing to be present, in witnessing my father's death, is what I needed to force the death of my strengths and weaknesses. In doing so, I gave myself permission to live beyond my life of pretension.

It's easy to pretend you don't need your parents. This is especially true for people who live without the benefit of a strong relationship with their parents. Sadly, many learn what not to do from their parents versus gaining from their promises. I get that.

My lessons aren't the consequence of a perfect relationship with my daddy. I continue to grapple with the absence of declarations of "I love you, son" to help me name what I feel. I've come to grips with how my daddy was shaped by a culture that understood manhood as what we do rather than what we say. The temptation is to be critical based on the paradigm of this generation. Knowing and understanding my daddy begins with doing more in understanding what he was forced to overcome.

There is something to be said about how so much of my daddy's living and being was a construction of pretension. Pretending to be strong was part of the faking it until you make it mentality that continues to impact the mental health of black men. Be it the faking that pops up in the formation of "thug" culture or the massive pretension exposed through overly lavish lifestyles aimed at painting the image of living that life – black men often live with the burden of hiding what they perceive to be weaknesses.

My daddy's promise attempted to lure me away from the seduction of proving manhood with stuff. This is part of the manipulation that keeps black men trapped within a vicious cycle of debt and manufactured manhood. Pretension obstructs movement toward legitimate manhood. Being that good man involves the promises my daddy extended throughout my life – take care of your wife and children, don't allow the views of others to impact how you treat them and don't judge people based on what you see.

Caregiving helped eradicate my massive pretension due to what was taken away. When the majority of a person's life is about fulfilling the will to play, it's easy to forfeit the balance needed to become a better man.

Lesson #2. Becoming my daddy's caregiver helped me understand, and move beyond, the realization that I'm the product of a culture that demands sacrifice to something greater than my own will to live and achieve.

I know. This sounds like a contradiction of the previous lesson. This is a lesson that demands an understanding of healthy balance. It's also a statement best understood within the context of cultural differences related to how black people approach caregiving.

Cross bearing is a central theological theme for black people. The assumption that picking up a cross, as a critical witness of faith, is taught and celebrated in ways that hinder positive mental health. Being present with and for a parent demands the type of balance that offsets notions of caregiving as an act of martyrdom. Caregiving is not a call to death. I'm suggesting it is an opportunity to learn and grow, which may demand a level of stripping, but death is not the intended goal.

My personal confession of my experience in caring for my daddy results in what feels like death. This is not a reflection of the doing as much as the mindset that went into the doing. My death was, in many ways, self-imposed and legitimized by my need to punish myself due to the guilt I felt as a result of not being present for many years.

I strongly recommend caregivers find support groups to help with the internalized pain. Please, do not travel down this road alone. Find and use all the help you can get.

Lesson #3. My willingness to become a caregiver is based on my understanding of life and ministry as a call to non-being.

This lesson is connected to Lesson #2. The work of caregiving can benefit from serious theological examination. So much of what we're taught about ministry is rooted in kenosis, the act of the self-emptying' of Jesus' own will in becoming entirely receptive of God's divine will. John of the Cross, the mystic theologian who wrote <u>Dark Night of the Soul</u>, utilized the teachings of Philippians 2:7 to explain God's process in transforming believers into the likeness of Christ.

Historically, kenosis is used to denote the ongoing self-denial of one's will and desire applied through self-sacrifice; leading to a person becoming holy. Caregivers should avoid the temptation of self-emptying for the sake of revealing a faith separating them from others.

Caregiving, theologically speaking, is not an act of self-emptying as much as it is about being present with a person in support of a mutually beneficial relationship. Caregiving is not only about what is lost; it is also about what is gained as a result of being present.

Lesson # 4. Being an effective caregiver requires freedom in maintaining the needs of the caretaker and caregiver.

I will say it again. Caregiving is a mutually beneficial relationship. Caregiving builds faith and understanding. People who engage in this work are best served by embracing what they gain versus feeling burdened by what is lost. What is lost is, in many ways, part of what is gained. The work of caregiving demands a spiritual focus aimed at elevating how a person conceptualizes the meaning of their life.

I use the word freedom as an intentional way to express how this work is a decision. We are free to engage in this work in ways that reflect the needs of both caretaker and caregiver. In choosing to focus on one without serious consideration related to how caregiving is a mutually beneficial relationship can lead to serious emotional distress. Caregivers are free to celebrate the benefits of caregiving while owning things lost as potential gifts.

Anyone who has walked down this path knows it's not simple. So much is lost. It is hard not to become consumed with regret. I've been there. Wait, I continue to live with all that was lost.

This is a statement about what I wish I had done versus all I did. Sure, there are the lessons that come after death. I learned things without knowing what I was learning. In other words, going through it helps once you're through it all. That may not help me, but the lessons are meant for those going through it now.

So, what do I suggest?

1. Begin by celebrating your decision. Don't begin by counting
   all that is lost. I did that, and it triggered massive depression.
   It helps me to celebrate getting to know more about
   my daddy.

1. What are you celebrating? A chance to learn more about
   yourself. Let's face it, we are an accumulation of childhood
   mess. We cover so much involving how we feel about our
   parents. Caregiving grants you an opportunity to deal with
   all that mess before it's too late There's no guarantee
   everything will be fixed, but you will depart knowing you
   did your best.

1. Part of that celebration involves giving yourself permission
   to love who you've become and who you are becoming.
   Don't be afraid to revisit your childhood. Face it, for real this
   time. Learn to love the emerging you in ways that move you
   toward the person beyond all that pain.

1. Write this stuff down. Get a journal. Write, write, write and
   don't edit how you feel. You deserve every word of how
   you feel.

1. Don't isolate. Find someone to discuss this with. Get a
   therapist. Get someone.

1. Take care of yourself. Find ways to share your life and love.

Don't apologize for needing a person in your life. Caregiving should never come with the sacrifice of your being a person who needs to give and receive love.

1. Don't blame God. Blame how God is misunderstood. Yes, I said it. Challenge theology that normalizes pain and sacrifice. God hasn't ordained a life of suffering. Seek joy, embrace it and celebrate God's work in your life.

1. Finally, get some help. I know, I already said it. Echo please. Don't do the work of caregiving by yourself. Give yourself permission to allow others to help you. If you seek them, they will appear.

WHAT DO you do when it's all over? I don't know.

IT'S NOT OVER YET. The aftermath of caregiving is, in many ways, harder than the caregiving. With all the lessons learned after the fact, I'm dealing the best I can because I failed to follow my own lessons. That sucks. I know.

I'm still doing the best I can to find my former self. I'm closer to concluding I'll never find him. He's lost forever. This is the new me. I like to think I'm an improved version. It's hard believing that when some of the stuff lost is needed. In other words, I can celebrate the part that is lost.

Finding and maintaining work has been tough.

Sleeping is even harder. I continue to fear my daddy falling in the middle of the night. The truth is I need someone to help pick me up. I keep falling and I don't know why.

With all of that said, my daddy's promises linger. I know, because of him, I'm a better man. He comes to me often. I'm grateful for my daddy's presence. I still miss him. I miss him even more when he's near. It sounds silly missing someone who's so near. The pain of his presence is part of the gift. It reminds me of my need to remember the promises while doing more to live with the lessons.

I'm left with all that was lost. My mama sold my daddy's house to the church that refused to allow us to have the funeral there. She sold the house for $17,000. The church robbed my mama of my daddy's property.

I'm still praying about that.

I returned home from a long trip to discover the house was consumed with black mold. That's one of the reasons my mama sold the house to the church next door. That and a tree fell on the house. The cost to repair the damage was more than we could afford. I can't blame my mama but going back home is no longer a possibility.

All my clothes were destroyed by the black mold. Starting over hasn't been easy. My daddy didn't leave me with an inheritance. I was left the cost to open and close the grave before his funeral. My daddy failed to think about that expense. I paid the $2,500 and did my best to make the pain go away. That's what people do after it's all over.

I placed everything I had in my Lincoln MKZ and headed back to Durham, North Carolina in August 2016. Things weren't the same at Bethel Church. I failed to consider the impact it all had on my mental health and the doing led to my making bad decisions. That's a lesson for another day. More people should talk about that. I may someday. Who knows? I wonder if anyone cares.

There's not much left, but I still have My Daddy's Promises.

That's the miracle of caregiving. I'm my daddy's son and, because of him, I'm a better man. I'm still working on it, but my daddy's lessons are with me to lead the way.

My Daddy Promised.

Can you hear him?

"I'm here son. Not going nowhere."

EPILOGUE

The tears keep coming. They may never go away. I'm cool with that.

It's what you do with the tears that matters. You can allow them to soak the soul until nothing is left but a puddle of misery. Or, you can use tears to nurture seeds for others to blossom.

There is a witness in tears. They remind us we are never alone. We all cry together. We cry in isolated corners, but there is comfort whenever we find one another to share the reason for the tears. The miracle of tears is when our crying together becomes Pentecost – like speaking in tongues, our wailing resurrects the comfort of many clouds of witnesses.

My tears conjure a new mission. The release of My Daddy's Promise: Lessons Learned in Caregiving begins a journey to find people challenged by their tears. Tears are a reminder that ministry is not about saving them. It is also about me. It is almost always about us. It is the work we do together and how the tears force deeper contemplation regarding the steps we take – together – when the tears don't go away.

My new mission is to find wailing servants. In finding them, my desire is to cry with them as a reminder of never being alone. Ministry isn't limited to my saving them from their sins. Only God can do that. I need them to save me from the pain of my tears. My strength is in their presence. Crying together is a reminder of our strength.

The word caregiver presupposes a posture of isolation. Giver. Just one. Alone. There's a singleness implied in the word that negates the essence of our communal witness. It refutes the significance of what it means to be a Christian. Our faith is built on the power of two or three gathering together. The word caregiver implies the burden of one person in comforting the agony of their tears.

Crying alone is what makes caregiving oppressive activity. Caregivers should never be left alone to cry. Caregiving is the transformative work of the resurrected Christ. As such, caregiving is the work we do in addressing the needs of family members we call the Church This is the work of the Church.

My mission is to evangelize the ministry of caregiving. There is something deeply sinful in faith communities neglecting the needs of caregivers. My challenge is for faith communities to envision ways to offer ministry for caregivers.

My Daddy's Promise: Lesson's Learned in Caregiving is more than my personal story of caregiving. It is about the tears I shed alone, but, even more, it relates the absence of the Church in providing hope and inspiration during and after my caregiving experience. The work of the Church involves wiping those tears. Caregiving is the work we do together.

With the release of My Daddy's Promise: Lessons Learned in Caregiving I embark on a journey across the country to share my story, cry with caregivers and challenge faith leaders and members of congregations to consider the ministry of caregiving. I imagine countless men and women crying alone. We notice their absence when the hardships of caregiving complicate their attendance. We see the names of the sick and shut-in placed in the church bulletin. Their names are uttered just before the congregation prays.

What about the names of caregivers?

Do we pray for caregivers as they do the work of ministry while crying alone?

The tears never go away.

Let us cry together as God wipes away our tears.

I.

CPSIA information can be obtained
at www.ICGtesting.com
Printed in the USA
JSHW041715230521
15077JS00004B/13

9 781734 732900